Street by Street

DARTFORD
GRAVESEND

CRAYFORD, SWANLEY, TILBURY

Eynsford, Greenhithe, Hartley, Hextable, Istead Rise, Meopham, New Ash Green, New Barn, Northfleet, South Darenth, Swanscombe, West Kingsdown

1st edition September 2002

© Automobile Association Developments Limited 2002

Ordnance Survey® This product includes map data licensed from Ordnance Survey® with the permission of the Controller of Her Majesty's Stationery Office. © Crown copyright 2002. All rights reserved. Licence No: 399221.

Published by AA Publishing (a trading name of Automobile Association Developments Limited, whose registered office is Millstream, Maidenhead Road, Windsor, Berkshire SL4 5GD. Registered number 1878835).

The Post Office is a registered trademark of Post Office Ltd. in the UK and other countries.

Schools address data provided by Education Direct.

One-way street data provided by:

Tele Atlas © Tele Atlas N.V.

Mapping produced by the Cartographic Department of The Automobile Association. A01100

A CIP Catalogue record for this book is available from the British Library.

Printed by GRAFIASA S.A., Porto, Portugal

Ref: ML175

Key to map pages	ii-iii
Key to map symbols	iv-1
Street by Street	2-53
Index – towns & villages	54
Index – streets	55-62
Index – featured places	63-64

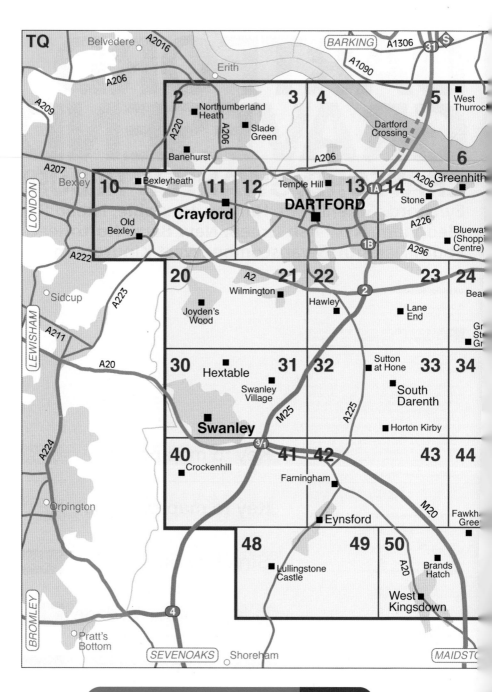

TQ

Belvedere A2016

Erith

BARKING A1306 31 S

A1090

A206

A209

A220

A206

A207

Bexley

LONDON

A222

Sidcup

LEWISHAM

A211

A20

A224

Orpington

BROMLEY

Pratt's
Bottom

SEVENOAKS Shoreham

2 Northumberland Heath	3	4		5 West Thurroc

2 Northumberland Heath
Slade Green
Banehurst

3

4

Dartford Crossing

5 West Thurroc

A206

6

10 Bexleyheath

Old Bexley

11 Crayford

12 Temple Hill

13 DARTFORD 1A **14** Stone

Greenhith

A206

A226

Bluewat (Shoppi Centre)

1B A296

20 A2

Joyden's Wood

21 Wilmington

22 Hawley

23 Lane End

24 Bea

Gr St Gr

2

A225

30 Hextable

31 Swanley Village

32 Sutton at Hone

33 South Darenth

34

Horton Kirby

M25

Swanley

3/1

40 Crockenhill

41

42 Farningham

Eynsford

43

44

M20

Fawkh Gree

A223

48 Lullingstone Castle

49

50 Brands Hatch

A20

West Kingsdown

4

MAIDST

Scale of map pages   1:15,000   4.2 inches to 1 mi

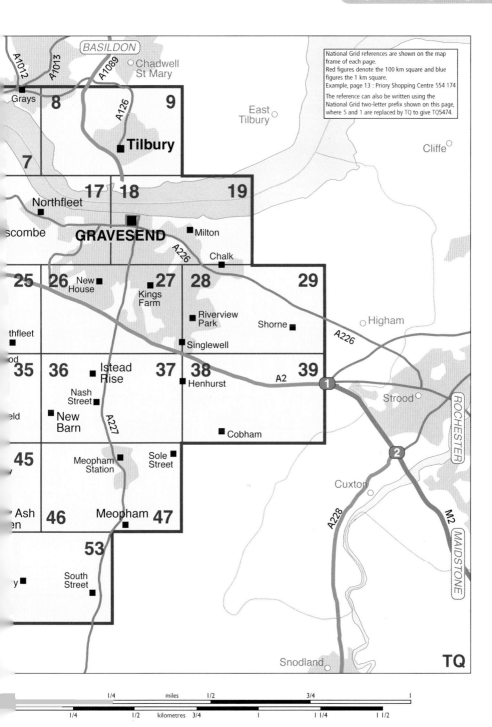

BASILDON

A1012 A1013 A1089 ○ Chadwell
St Mary

A126

Grays   **8**   **9**   East ○
                                    Tilbury

■ **Tilbury**   Cliffe ○

7

17 18   **19**

Northfleet

scombe **GRAVESEND**   ■ Milton

                A226   Chalk ■

25 **26** New ■   **27** **28**   **29**
            House
                     Kings
                     Farm
                                                      ○ Higham
                          ■ Riverview
                            Park   Shorne ■
thfleet ■   A226
od   ■ Singlewell

35 **36** Istead ■ **37** **38**   A2   **39**
                Rise   ■ Henhurst   ①
            Nash   Strood ○
            Street ■   ROCHESTER
eld   ■ **New**   A227
       Barn
                                   ■ Cobham   ②
45   Meopham ■   Sole ■
            Station   Street   Cuxton ○

Ash **46** Meopham **47**   A228   M2
en   MAIDSTONE
       53

y ■   South
      Street ■

                                                      Snodland ○   **TQ**

National Grid references are shown on the map
frame of each page.
Red figures denote the 100 km square and blue
figures the 1 km square.
Example, page 13 : Priory Shopping Centre 554 174

The reference can also be written using the
National Grid two-letter prefix shown on this page,
where 5 and 1 are replaced by TQ to give TQ5474.

	miles		
1/4		1/2	3/4	1

| 1/4 | 1/2 | kilometres 3/4 | 1 | 1 1/4 | 1 1/2 |

iv

Junction 9	Motorway & junction	⊖	Underground station
Services	Motorway service area	⊖	Light railway & station
	Primary road single/dual carriageway	++++++++++	Preserved private railway
Services	Primary road service area	LC	Level crossing
	A road single/dual carriageway	•—•—•—•	Tramway
	B road single/dual carriageway	-----------	Ferry route
	Other road single/dual carriageway	....	Airport runway
	Minor/private road, access may be restricted	▬ ▪ ▪ ▪ ▪	County, administrative boundary
← ←	One-way street	▼▼▼▼▼▼▼▼▼	Mounds
	Pedestrian area	17	Page continuation
============	Track or footpath		River/canal, lake, pier
■■■■■■■■ ■■■■■■■■	Road under construction		Aqueduct, lock, weir
⊦- - - =⊣	Road tunnel	465 ▲ Winter Hill	Peak (with height in metres)
AA	AA Service Centre		Beach
P	Parking		Woodland
P+🚌	Park & Ride		Park
🚌	Bus/coach station		Cemetery
	Railway & main railway station		Built-up area
⇌	Railway & minor railway station		

	Featured building		Abbey, cathedral or priory
	City wall		Castle
A&E	Hospital with 24-hour A&E department		Historic house or building
PO	Post Office	Wakehurst Place NT	National Trust property
	Public library		Museum or art gallery
i	Tourist Information Centre		Roman antiquity
	Petrol station Major suppliers only		Ancient site, battlefield or monument
†	Church/chapel		Industrial interest
	Public toilets		Garden
	Toilet with disabled facilities		Arboretum
PH	Public house AA recommended		Farm or animal centre
	Restaurant AA inspected		Zoological or wildlife collection
	Theatre or performing arts centre		Bird collection
	Cinema		Nature reserve
	Golf course	V	Visitor or heritage centre
▲	Camping AA inspected		Country park
	Caravan Site AA inspected		Cave
	Camping & caravan site AA inspected		Windmill
	Theme park		Distillery, brewery or vineyard

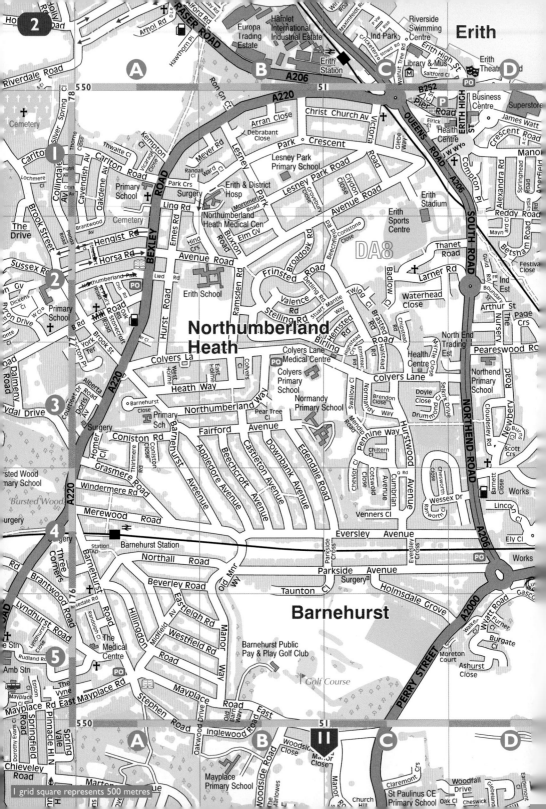

E   F   G   H

53   54   78

Lane   Way

Darent Industrial Park

Dayton Drive

Maypole Crescent

Burnett Road

Ness Road

Works

I

Works

Manford Industrial Estate

Ray Lamb Way

Bilton Road

Canada Road

Durian Way

M Cl   Pipe Cl   W Cl   S Cl   Jenningtree Rd   Sandpipe Dr   Beacon Rd   Widgeon Rd

Longreach

Gra Wy

Sheppey Cl

Alderney

Wallhouse Road

2

77

Slade Green Primary School

Road

Hilden Dr   Brompton Dr

Sns

Green   Road

W Cl

Hollywood Wy

Fern Cl

Larkswood Cl

Hazel Dr

Hazel

Rodeo Cl

Darent Valley Path

Joyce Green Lane

3

Bridge Plantation   Birch Plantation   te

Forest Road

Elm Road

Hazel Road

Willow   Road

Cedar Rd

Leycroft Gdns

Slade Green FC

Crayford Marshes

4

h

PO

Slade Green Station

Moat   Lane

Clark Cl

Oak Rd

Slade Green

Howbury Lane

Works

wbury Rd

Kent County

Bexley

4

176

Crayside Industrial Estate

Kennet Road

5

THAMES

ROAD

Maiden Lane

Thames Road

ur Rd   Shuttle Cl

y Road   Baurt Cl

Russel Cl

Works

A206

A206

Darent Valley Path

s C   ry School

Mayplace Avenue

Sandpit Road

Swan Business Park

n Mill Lane   Mill Place

rey Beech Walk   Stanham   orth

Crayside Industrial ate

A206

DA1

Shirley

Millside Industrial Estate

Barnes

Burnham

4

A   B   C   D

Works

Purfleet Station

Beacon Hill Industrial Estate

Botany Way

Hill

Harrisons Wharf

LC

A1090

LONDO

Thames

55

Purfleet

Maypole Crescent

ndau Way

strial

1

Long Reach

2

Dartford Marshes

Joyce Green Lane

y Path

3

3

4

Marsh Street

Marsh Street

5

A206   **UNIVERSITY WAY**

McCudden Rd

Grove Nest Rd

Cornwall Rd

Salmon Rd

Atlas Rd

A206   UNIVERSITY WY

Darent Valley Path

Joyce Green Lane

Strickland Av

Sharp Way

Strickland

Barnwell Rd

W Rd

Cemetery

A   B   **13**   C   D

Chaucer Wy

Wodehouse Road

Henderson Drive

Wordsworth Way

Byron

Cavell Crescent

Coleridge Rd

Lane

Wellcome A

Hall Road

Spielman Road

Berg Rd

Green Rd

Bronte Gv

Browning Road

Gv

54

77

76

78

554

554

55

55

Fleet By-Pass

E F G H

Joslin Rd
Linden Cl
Lockyer Rd
ROAD PURFLEET

57

A1090 STONEHO

Works

Weston

Eastern Av

The Glade
Business
Centre

Quarry

Works

158

Mother

Mn La

Fifth Av

Fourth Av

Third Av

Fifth Avenue
Second Av

Motherwell W
First Avenue

Road

London
Business Centre

Bay
Breach
Road

Thurrock

Bridge View
Industrial Est

S

I
PO

Hotel

Tunnel
Industrial
Estate

LC

LC

Works

Works

CANTERBURY WAY — A282(T)

A282(T)

Oliver Close

Works

Oliver Road

2

Ol

77

Works

Burnley Road

Watson Close

Oliver Road

3

6

Works

Dartford
Tunnel

Queen Elizabeth II
Bridge

4

176

A282(T)

5

Thurroc
Kent Cou

Bridge Close

Clipper Bvd
West

Stone
Marshes

Clipper

Bvd

A282(T)

CROSSWAYS BVD

E F G H

14

57

Hotel

58

Toll
Victory Way

Anchor Boulevard

Galleon

ton's

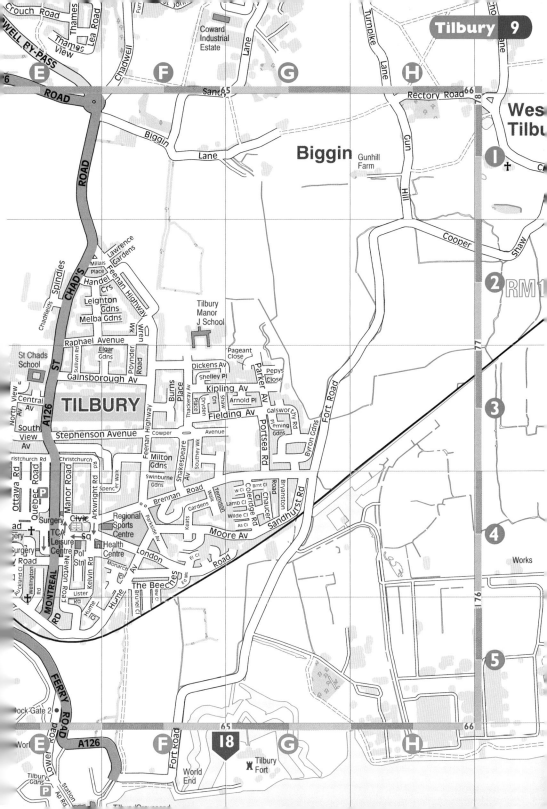

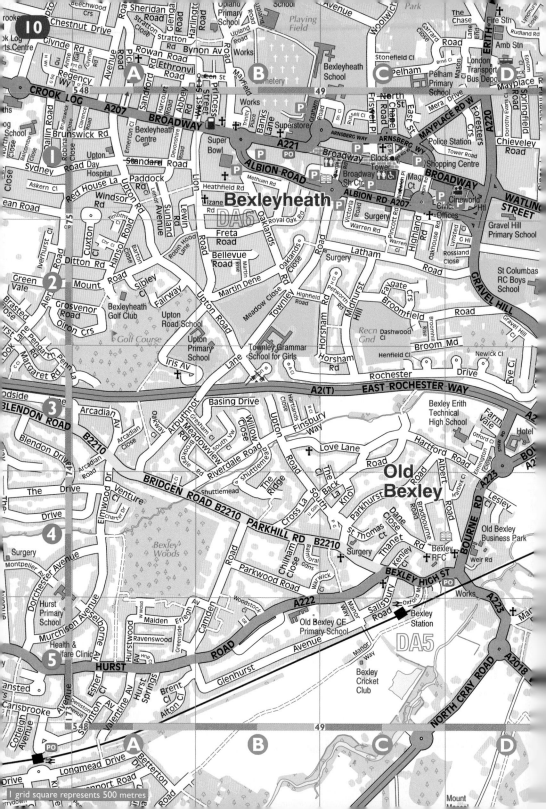

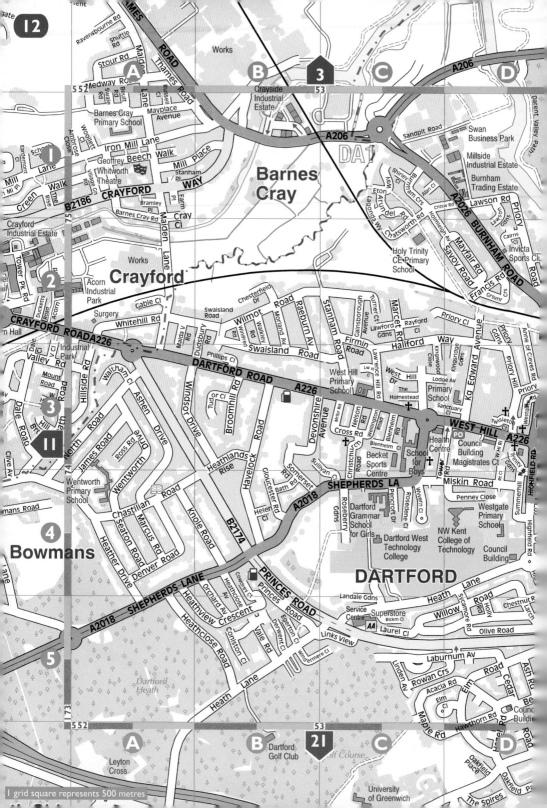

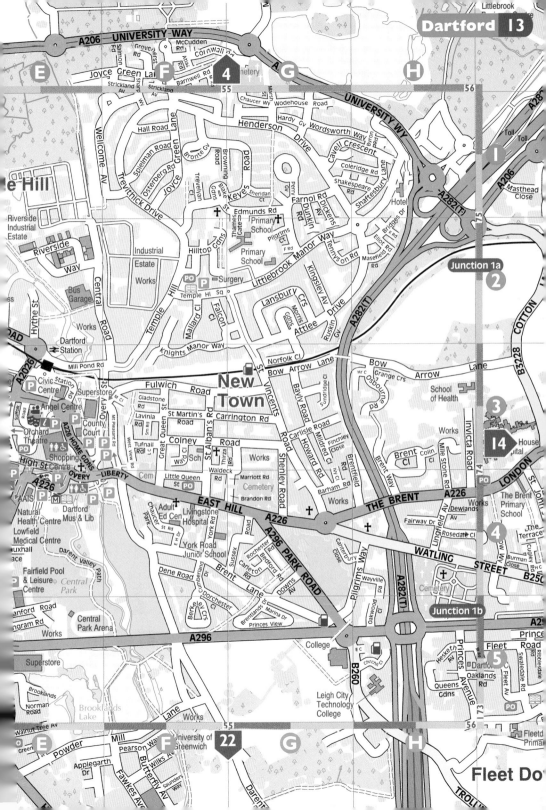

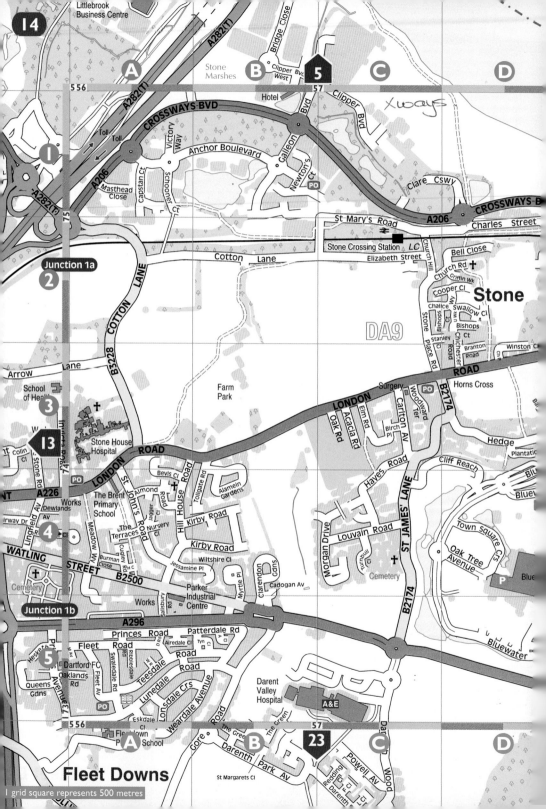

Thurrock
Kent County

E F 6 G H

59 60

I

Manor Way

Sara Crs
Frobishet Wy
Pier
HIGH STREET
King Edward Rd
Superstore
STATION RD
C V
Fiddlers Cl
B255
Road
Works

LONDON ROAD

Kestner Industrial Est
Eagles
Woodland Wy
Hillcrest Dr
Smugglers
Maritime Cl
Beaton
LONDON RD A226
Craylands Lane
Cr Sq
Swan Busi

Chambers Cl
Avenue
Low Cl
KG Edward Rd
Castle St
Evans Cl
providence St
A206
Station Road
A226
Greenhithe for Bluewater Stn
Park Terrace
PO
Knockhall
Greenhithe Health Clinic
Surgery
Greenhithe
Breakneck Hill
Bean Road
Mounts Road
The Crs
Port Av
Lane Av
Knockhall Chase
Evnsford Rd
Abbey Rd
Knockhall Road
Alexander Rd
Wakefield Rd
Dial Rd
Atlantic Cl
Pentstemon
2
Broomfield

Craylands La
Lewis
Milton
3
Moore Rd
Broad Rd
Gunn R
Jubilee Cl
Vale
Spring
Valley Vw
Guns
Kemsley Cl
Western Cross Cl
Hasted Cl
Whites Cl
View
Pilgrims
Alkerden Lane
Gilbert Cl
Childs Crs
Milton St
16
Alamein Av
Bo
Manor
Stone Castle
Mounts Road
Mounts Road
Manor Rd
Durrant Way
Manor Way
Leonard
4

P
Way
P
B255
P
Lime Tree Av
P
5

173

E F G H

59 60

ROMA 24 AD Works

Bean Lane

A296

A2(T)

A2(T)

A **B** 7 **C** **D**

560 61 Manor

1

Manor Way

Pilgrims' Road

Craylands Lane

LONDON ROAD A226

75

Kent Kraft Industrial Estate

Northfleet Industrial Estate

Northfleet Industrial Estate

Northfleet Industrial Estate

Works

Lower Rd

Works

Road

GALLEY HILL ROAD

Swanscombe Business Centre

Galley Hill Industrial Estate

Atlantic Cl

Pentstemon Drive

Pacific Cl

Broomfield Rd

Orchard Rd

All Saints Cl

B259 HIGH STREET

PO

Swanscombe Station

Taunton Road

Grove Road

Ebbsfleet Industrial Estate

Eagle

Railway St

Mann Rd

STONEBRIDGE ROAD

Park Wallis

College Road

Warwick Ct

Rose St

Rd Cr

2

DA10

The Grove

Swanscombe

Milton Road

Hope Rd

STANHOPE RD

Harmer Rd

Albert Rd

Herbert Rd

Surgery

Northfleet Station

Station Road

Craylands La

Milton St

Lewis Rd

Ames Rd

Moore Rd

Sweyne Rd

Stanley Rd

Gasson Rd

Church Road

B259

3

Trebble Road

Broad Rd

Park Road

Cemetery

Eglinton Rd

Castle Rd

Castle Rd

Vernon Road

Burns Road

15

Manor Rd

Alamein Rd

Bodle Av

Gunn Road

Rectory Rd

Beasnant Rd

St Paul's

Manor Rd

Boleyn Way

Seymour Rd

St Peter's Cl

Swanscombe Street

Milford Dr

Keary Road

Swan Valley Community School

under construction

4

Durrant Way

Leonard Avenue

The Sweyne Junior School

5

SOUTHFLEET ROAD

173

560 61

A **B** 25 **C** B259 **D**

Spring Head

E   F   8   G   H
63   64

Main Dock   Dock Gate

Works

Tilbury
Ness

I

Tilbury
Gdns

75

Lond
Cruis

2   Thu
                     Kent

The Shore

Clifton Marine
Pde

Northfleet

Works

Rosherville

The Shore

Imperial
Business
Est

Clifton Marine
Parade

Superstore

Lawn Primary
School

Gravesend &
Northfleet FC

Lansdowne Sq

East
Mill

West Mill

Supe

Pier Road

Granby Road

Crete

Hall

Road

Works

Fountain
Walk

Cross Rd

Thames Way

Imp
Ret
Par

3

Portland
Road

Rosherville
Way

Works

St Marina Dr

74

Super

CLIFFE

Hotel

The Shore

The HILL

Surgery

A226   LONDON   ROAD

Rosherville
CE Primary
School

St Mark's Av

St James's Avenue

18

St Jam
Road

Bro
Sch

Church
Pth

Laburnum Gv

Lime Avenue

Robinia Av

Plane Av

Rosherville
Wy

Rural Vale

Mill Rd

Gordon Road

Burnaby Rd

Beresford Rd

PO

A2260

Vauxhall Cl

Surgery

Grange Road

4

B2175

B261

Shepherd St

York Rd

St Botolphs
CE Primary
School

Dudely
Road

Beaumont Dr

Beaumont Rd

Lennox Road

Lennox Rd

Perry Street

SPRINGHEAD RD

Tooley St

DOVER   ROAD

Vale Road

Detling Rd

THAMES WAY

St Josephs
RC School

DA11

Council
Building

A2260

Preston Rd

First Av

Coulton Av

Dover Road
Primary School

Fiveash Rd

Stanbrook Rd

Mayfield Rd

Campbell Road

Granville Road

Pelham Road

Gravesend School
for Girls

5

OLD ROAD

Primary School

Napier Road

Cecil Road

SPRINGHEAD ROAD

Cemetery

Haldane Gardens

Camden Gdns

PO

Waterdales

The Old
Guild Theatre

Northfleet
School
for Boys

Couge Av

Davis Av

Park

Vale

Foxwood Gv

Rosebank Gdns

Tudor Road

Perry St

Saintsbury

Brook Rd

May Avenue
Industrial
Est

EAST

May Av

Victoria Rd

Glebe
Road

Churchill Rd

Pelham Rd

Northcote Rd

Salisbury Road

Seymour Rd

Bedford Rd

Cemetery

63

Cygnet
Leisure
Centre

Perry St

Surg

Earl Road

Alfred
Place

Cooper's
Road

64

E   F   26   G   H

Hall Road

Wombwell
Gdns

Millfield Dr

Coldham

Hardy Av

Shelling Avenue

Beatrice Gdns

Miroy Avenue

Newman's Rd

The Crse

Hardy Avenue

strutto

Hartshill Road

Newton Abbot Road

Downage

Farmcroft

Grid reference: **18**

Grid columns: A, B, **9** (65), C, D (top); A, B, **27**, C, D (bottom)
Grid rows: I, 2, 3, **I7**, 4, 5

Key labels and features (left to right, top to bottom):

Dock Gate 2 · 564 · 65
FERRY ROAD · A126 · Tower Road · Station Ap Rd
Works · Tilbury Gdns · Fort Road
World End · Tilbury Fort
London International Cruise Terminal · Tilbury/Gravesend Passenger Ferry

Gravesend Reach · River

Thurrock / Kent County

GRAVESEND

Royal Terrace Pier · Gravesend Rowing Club · Gravesend Yacht Club
Arts Centre · Royal Pier Road · Clarendon · Saxon Shore Way · Commercial · Gordon Pro
Clifton Marine Pde · Clifton Marine Parade · Superstore · WEST ST · CROOKED LA · THE TER · The Chantry · Custom House · Canal · Canal Basin
East Mill · West Mill · Pier Road · Thames Wy · Superstore · STUART RD · BATH ST · Magistrates Court · Terrace St · Milton Pl · Pilots Rd · Works · Russell Rd · Suffolk
St Georges · Anglesea Museum · Princess St · EMB · HARMER ST · Industrial Estate · Albion Road · Augustine · Norfolk Rd · St John's · Prospect
OVERCLIFFE · Imperial Retail Park · Council Building · New Rd · Bentley St · Ordnance Rd · Park Place · Albion Ter
Hotel · Lennox Av · Gravesend Stn · Cncl Bldg · LORD ST · Clock Tower · PO · Saddington St · Milton Road Business Park · Sch · Prospect · MILTON ROAD E
St James's Road · Bronte School · Rathmore Rd · Cobham St · Eden St · Gu'Nanak Sports Club · Alanbrooke · Craig Gdns · Church Wk
Surgery · Grange Road · Council Building · Darnley St · Spencer St · Cutmore St · Brandon · Cambrian · Parrock Street · Wellington Street · School · Trinity Rd · Armoury Dr · RW · Artillery · Donald Biggs Drive
Perry Street · Lennox Rd E · Arthur St · Clifton Rd · Williams Rd · Windmill St · Clarence Row · Home · Fleetway Sports Club · Bronte VW · Townfield · Pine
Campbell Road · Pelham Rd · The Avenue · Trafalgar Road · Surgery · Gravesend Cricket Club · Windfield · William · Temple · South Hl · Shrubbery · Park Av · Joy Rd · Milton Hall Road · Avenue
Granville Road · Lennox Rd · Kent Road · School · Clarence Pl · Sikh · Wrotham Road Health Clinic · Leith Pk · Glen View · South Hl Av · Parrock Avenue · Whitehall Rd · Laurel Rd · Hillside
Glebe Rd · OLD ROAD WEST · Darnley Rd · Essex Road · Portland Rd · Elmfield Cl · Rouge · Bank · Constitution · Convent Preparatory School · Hillside Drive
Pelham Rd · Northcote Rd · Cecil Rd · Salisbury Rd · Primary School · Bartlett Rd · Lynton Rd S · Pinnock's Av · Woodfield · Devonshire Rd · B261 · OLD R · Park Road · Leith Park · South HI View · Townfield Chr · The Yews · OLD ROA
Napier Road · Seymour Road · Bedford · Hartshill · Newton Road · Nelson Road · Downage · The Square · Cemetery · Hotel · St Thomas's · Trosley Av · Cross Lane W · Alfred Road · Mead Rd · Lennox Rd · Portland Avenue · Cross Lane · St Mary's Cl · Coombe Rd · Laurel Rd · Ferndale Rd · Hillside Ave · Lingfield Av · The Sandh

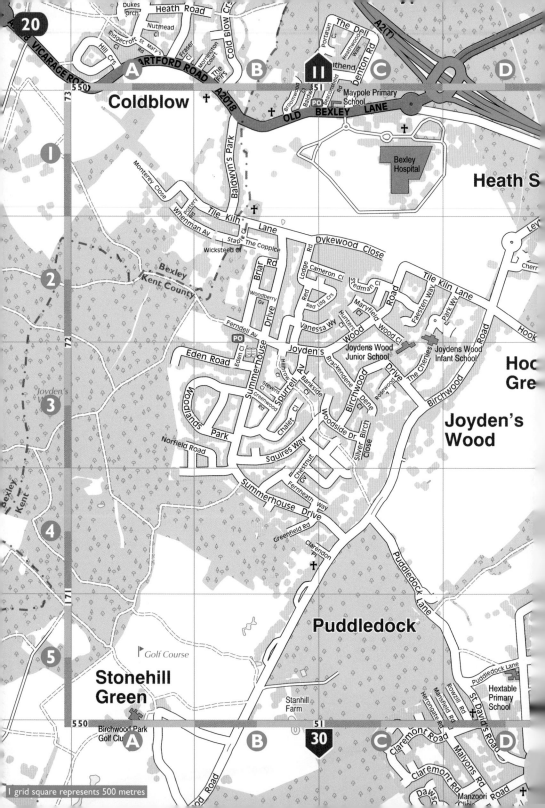

20

VICARAGE ROAD

73

Coldblow

HARTFORD ROAD   A2018   OLD   BEXLEY   LANE

Heath Road
Dukes Orch.
Nutmead Cl
St Mary's Rd
Ridgecroft Cl
Hill Crs
Fraser Cl
Mornington Court
The Firs
Blow Cr
Clow

Portanan
The Dell
Heathwood Walk
Southend
Denton Rd
Broomwood
Baldwyn
Beaconsfield
PO
Maypole Primary School

A2(T)

51

A   **B**   II   **C**   **D**

I

Monterey Close
Pottery
Whenman Av
Tile Kiln
Baldwyn's Park
Lane
Staple
Wicksteel Cl
The Coppice

Bexley
Kent County

Dykewood Close

Tile Kiln Lane

Lev
Cher

Heath S

2

72

Briar
Rd
Woodberry Gv
Ferndell Av
PO
Eden Cl
Eden Road
Summerhouse
Lodge Rd
Cameron Cl
Red Red Log Crs
Vanessa Wy
Stedman
Maryfield
Hunters
Wood Cl
Wood
Brackendene
Joyden's
Joydens Wood Junior School
Faesten Way
Park Wy
The Cherries
Joydens Wood Infant School
Road
Tile Kiln Lane
Birchwood
Road

Hook

Hoc
Gre

3

Joyden's Wood

Woodlands Park
Norfield Road
Steven
Greenwood Rd
Hill Crs
Spurrell
Av
Bankside
Chalet Cl
Squires Way
Woodside Dr
Dene Cl
Birchwood
Rosewood
Silver Birch
Close
Drive

Joyden's Wood

4

Bexley Kent

711

Chestnut Gv
Fernheath Way
Summerhouse Drive
Greenfield Rd
Clarendon Pl

Puddledock

Puddledock Lane

5

Golf Course

Stonehill Green

550

Birchwood Park Golf Clu

Stanhill Farm

30

51

Puddledock Lane
Hermongate Rd
Rowhill Rd
Mansfield Rd
St David's Rd
Hextable Primary School

Claremont Road
Malyons Rd
Claremont Rd
Dawso

Manzoori Clinic

A   **B**   **C**   **D**

Princes Road
Road
Airedale Cl
Road
Teesdale
Swaledale Rd
Ribblesdale
Road
FC Fleet Av
Lunedale
Lonsdale Crs
Weardale Avenue

A296

Darent
Valley
Hospital

PO E

Eskdale
Cl

Fleetdown
Primary School

F

14

G

H

I

The Green

Gore Road

Darenth Park Av

St Margarets Cl

The Green

Powell Av

Redding
Darenth Park Av

Darenth Wood Road

Cemetery

et Downs

OWN HILL B260

A2(T)

Darenth
Wood

Wood Lane

72

2

3

24

Lords
Wood

GREEN STREET GREEN ROAD

Coombfield Drive

Sinclair Way

Bennett Wy

PO

Moss Wy

Surgery

Lordswood
Cl

Collier
Crs

Langlands Dr

Court Rd

St Lukes Cl

Darenth Wood Road

Ladywood Road

4

**Lane
End**

Hill

Hill Rise

Hillside

Ridgeway

Stevens Cl

B260

Darenth

Darent Valley Path

Darenth
Primary
School

Road

171

5

Gree
Gree

E

Roman Villa Road

F

33

Margaret's

St

G

Road

H

St Margaret's

57

58

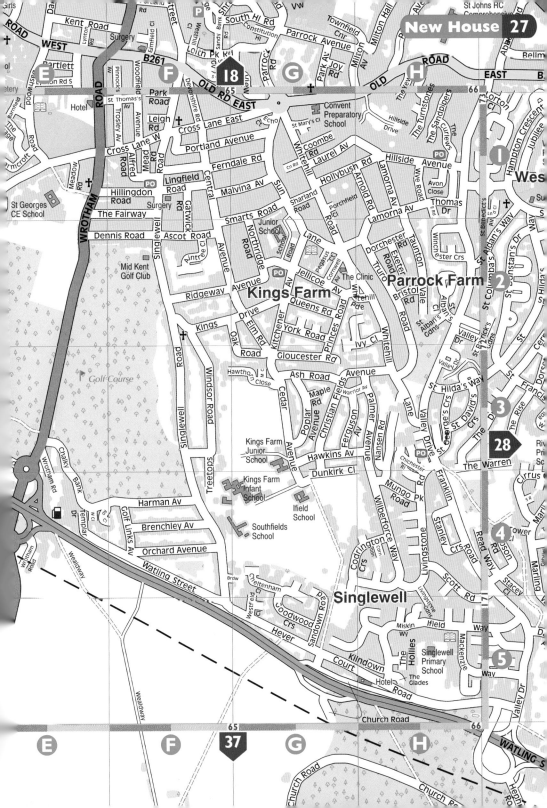

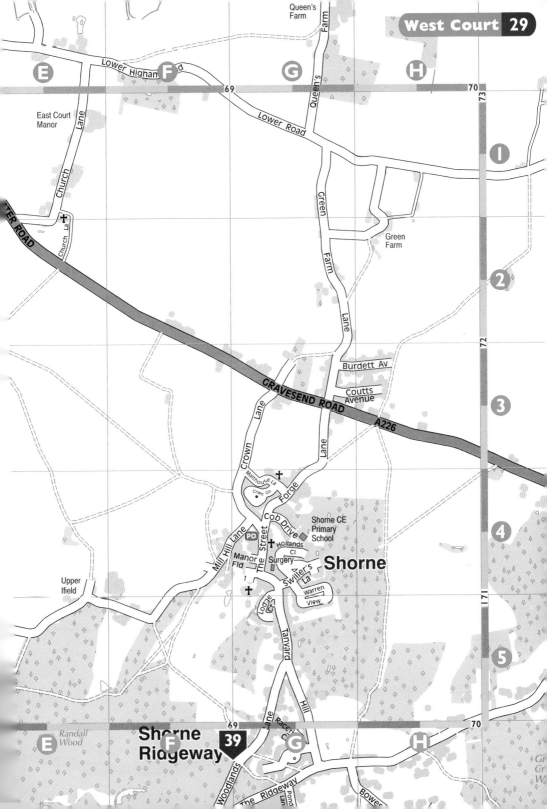

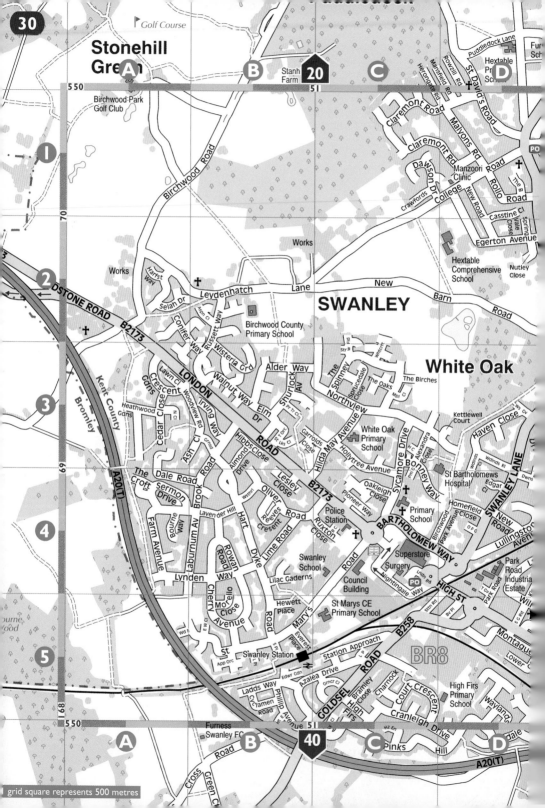

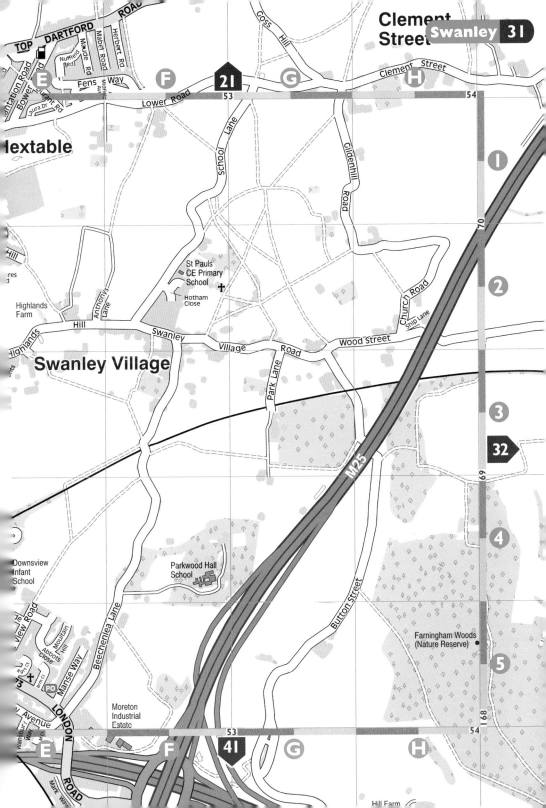

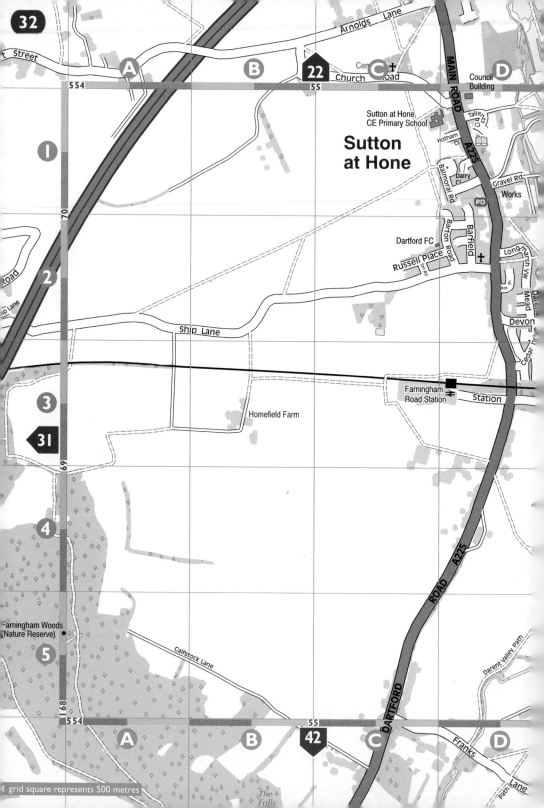

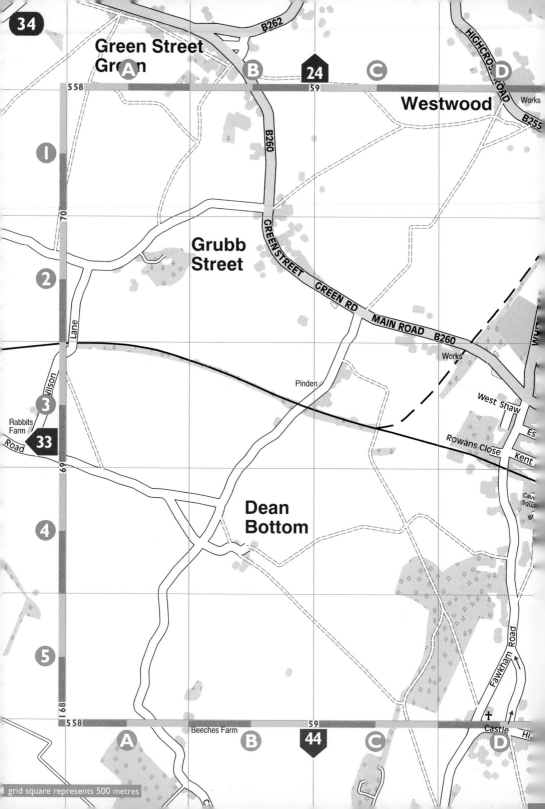

36

Gloxinia Road

A   B   **26**   C   D

562   63

I

70

Broad   Ditch   Road

Istead Rise

Fairview Road

Burghfie
Rd
Northumberland Rd
Brookside Rd

The Knole

Flowerhill

H Wy

Littlecroft

Weald Cl

Hill Cl

The Drove Way

Worcester Cl

Crockenhall Way

Biddenden Way

Longwalk

Upper Avenue

Elwill Way

Lewis Road

Castlefields

Lesley Close

Istead Ris

Hav Close

2

PO

Downs Road

Lyndhurst Way

Arcadia Road

Rosegarth

Istead Rise
Primary School

Chequers
Close

Downs Road

New Barn

Studley Crescent

Ridgewood

New Barn Road

Birch Close

Foxwood Way

Nash Bank

3

Street

A1

Haw

Hawl

Longfield

Yew Tree Cl

Walnut Hill Road

A2

35

Beverley Cl

The Gables

Poplars Close

Deerhurst Cl

Avenue

New Barn Road

Kenwood Avenue

Woodlea

Woodland Close

Festival Avenue

Greenways

North Riding

Nurstead Avenue

Ladwings

Greenfinches

The Hollies

Fawkham

The Oval

Avenue

Weird Wood

The Laurels

Ferndene

Barnfield Close

Selbourne Close

Stony Corner

4

View Road

Hill

Fairlight Cross

The Yews

The Old

Pincroft

Fairlight Cross

Wood

Park   Hill

5

MAIN ROAD   B260

Nurstead   Lane

Nurstead Hill
Farm

**Longfield
Hill**

562   168

63

Ryecroft

PO

A   B   **46**   C   D

Manor

Road

Birt
Jo

ORCHARD

1 grid square represents 500 metres

E   F   **27**   G   H

65   Church Road   66

Church Road

Kilndown
Court

The
Glades

School

Way

Hotels

Valley Dr

WATLING ST

Wealdway

Church Road

Church Road

I

Henhurst
Road

Church Rd

70

2

Henh

Henhurst Road

Wealdway

Church Road

3

Jeskyns Farm

38

Jeskyns Road

4

sh
eet

Round Street

**Round
Street**

Wealdway

Copt Hall Road

Round Street

t

ad Church Lane

5

White Post Lane

The
Beeches

168

E   F   **47**   G   H

65   66

Meopham
Stati

Sole
Street

ation
oad

Edmund Cl

dva Rd

ry Road

Sallows Shaw

Manor Road

Manor Ct

Scratton Fields

Street

Green Lane

Gold Street

Meopham

PO

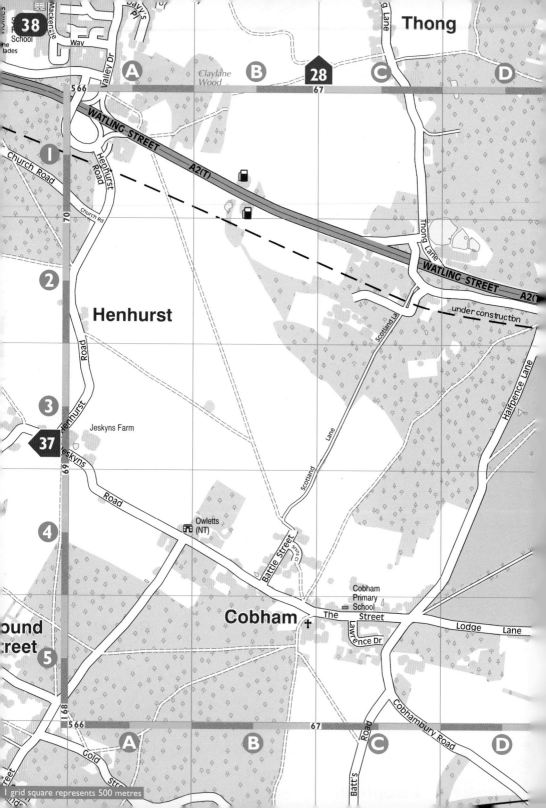

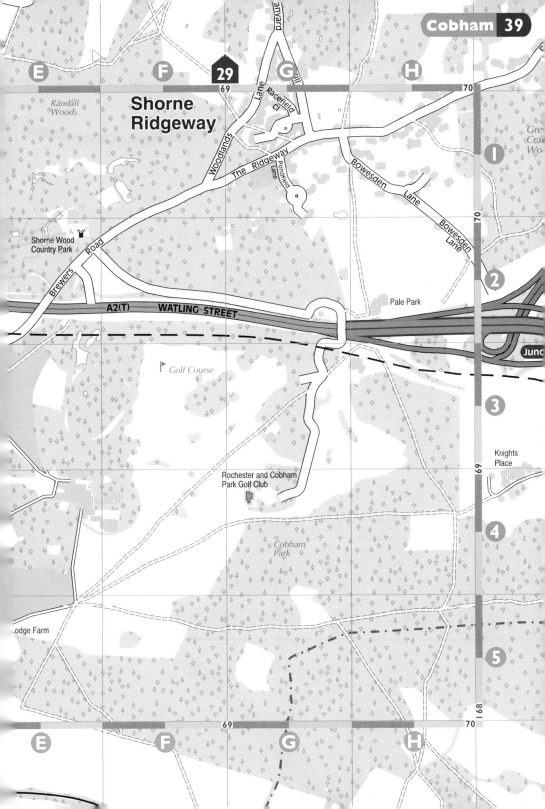

E   F   G   H

29
69

Shorne Ridgeway

Randall Wood

Woodlands

Racefield Cl

Lane

The Ridgeway

Pondfield Lane

Bowesden Lane

Bowesden Lane

I

70

Shorne Wood Country Park

Brewers Road

2

A2(T)   WATLING STREET

Pale Park

Junc

Golf Course

3

Knights Place

69

Rochester and Cobham Park Golf Club

4

Cobham Park

odge Farm

5

68

70

69

E   F   G   H

E
Manse Way
Beecher
London
PO

Moreton Industrial Estate

F

31

53

G

H

54 68

Wansbury Way
M Cl

Mark Way

LONDON
ROAD

I

Pedham Place Industrial Estate

Lane

Teardrop Industrial Park

Hill Farm

Farningham Hill Rd

Junction 3/1

LONDON ROAD

2

67

Wested Lane

Crockenhill Lane

3

42

4

166

Anthony F Primary S

Eynsford Castle

Hulberry

Darent Valley Path

5

Eynsford Cricket Club

Riverside

Lane

Home Farm

A225

E

F

48

53

G

H

54

PO
PH

STATION ROAD

Saddler's Park

Pollyhaugh

Darent

Kirby

Lombard Street
Foc
Chu
Pashleigh Way
Carleton Pl

E F **33** G H

57 58 68

Reynolds Place

ill

Mussenden Farm

ton Pl

ne Farm

I

Mussenden Lane

School Lane

2

67

Gates Road

3

44

Horton Wood

4

66

M20

Speedgate

Gabrielspring Rd

Gabriel Spring Road (East)

Speed Gate

5

GORSE

57 58

E F **50** G H

Scr s Lane

HILL

olin Chapman Way

Sun

44

558
68

A   B   **34**   C   D

59

Fawkham Road

Castle Hill

Beeches Farm

1

Canada Farm Road

Scudders Hill

67

C
S
Cl

Court
Lodge

2

Manor Lane

Three Gates Road

3

orton
ood

43

Grove
Farm

Valley Road

Fawkham
CE Primary
School

Fawkham
Manor

4

Fawkham
Manor Hospital

66

Speedgate Hill

5

Spee
Gate

Sun

Hill

Valley Rd

Michaels

Lane

Butchers

558

hapman Way

PH

PO

Small
Gr

A   B **Fawkh** m   **51**   C   D
               Green   **West Yo**

59

Fawkham

Beech

1 grid square represents 500 metres

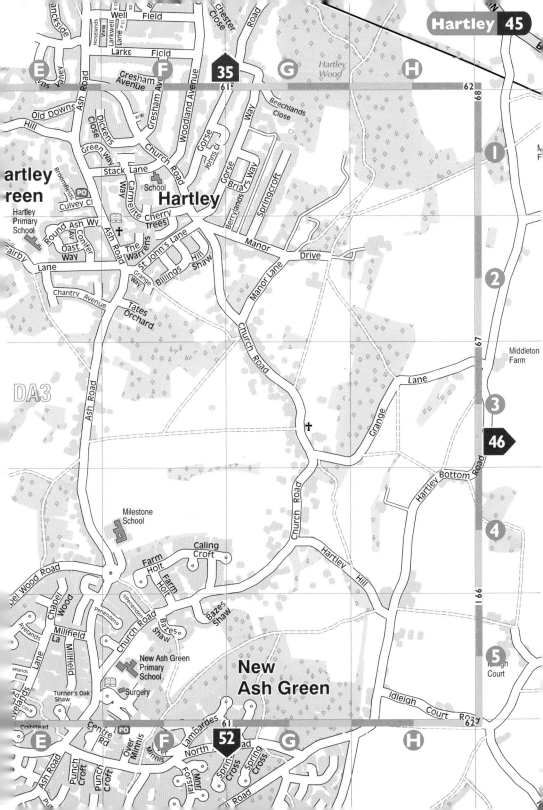

46

B260

N ROAD

Nurstead Lane

Nurstead Hill Farm

Longfield Hill

A

B

36

C

D

562

68

63

Birtrick

Orchard Drive

John

1

Manor Farm

Manor Road

Ryecroft

PO

2

67

Longfield Road

Melliker

Me

A

Lane

Middleton Farm

3

45

Hartley Bottom

Road

4

Shipley Hills

M

166

5

Idleigh Court

h Court Road

562

A

B

53

C

D

63

1 grid square represents 500 metres

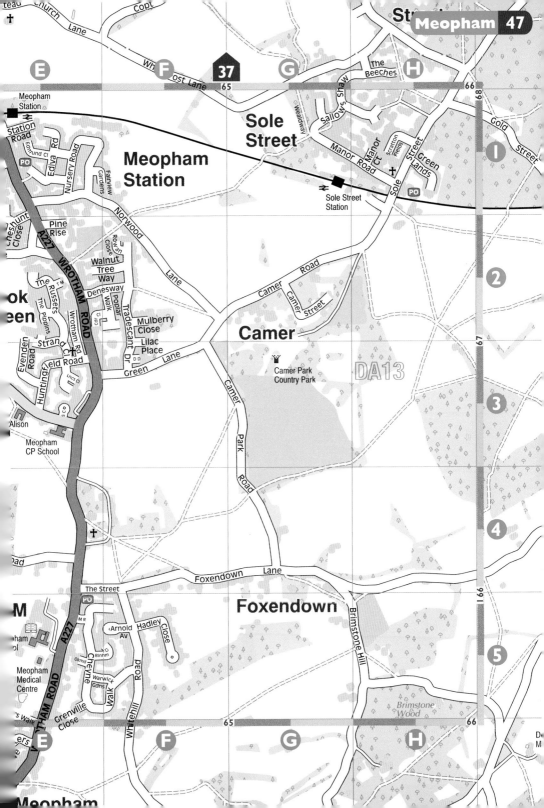

Hulberry

A 552 B 53 **41** C Lane D

Darent Valley Path

Riversid

Home Farm

STATION ROAD

A225

St Martins Dr

Lullingstone

1
65

Darent Valley Path

Lullingstone
Roman Villa

Birch Close

Eynsford Rise

2

Lullingstone
Park Farm

A225

Eynsford
Station

Lullingstone
Park

3
64

Darent Valley Path

Lullingstone
Castle

Upper

Austin

Chall

echen
ood

Lodge

Lower Austin
Lodge

4

Castle Road

Castle Farm

The
Birches

Lane

5

Road

1 63

552 53

A B C D

Farm

Darent Valley

Preston Farm

1 grid square represents 500 metres

EYNSFORD

E F **42** G H

55 56

Tow
Croft

A225 HIGH St.

ord
ford
el.

Bower Lane

Pollyhaugh
Farm

Maplescombe Lane

I

65

2

Park
House

Maplescombe

3

50

64

Bower
Park Farm

4

Bower Lane

Hog
Wood

5

163

55 56

E F G H

Upper
Austin Lodge

n Lodge
Club

High
Castle
Wood

50

556

A   GORSE   **B**   **43**   **C**   **D**

Gabrielspring Rd   Gabriel Spring Road (East)   Spee Gate

M20

57

Scratchers Lane

I

65

A20   HILL

Colin Chapm

Works

2

Grandstand

Brands Hatch
Motor Racing Circuit

3

49

64

Kingsdown
Farm

Symonds
Close

Road

Gillies
Road

Viking   Way

4

Botsom

Blue
Chalet
Ind Park

Phelps   St Cl
Cl

Neal

Oaklands Cl

LC

Brakes
Place

Avenue

Regency
Close

Millfield

Sherbourne
Close

Road

Knatts

Lane

The Briars

Hever
Rd

Hever

Multon

Astor Rd

Hever Wood Road

PO

Hwlls Cl

Whtgt Av

W V Cl

Mitchem Cl

5

Valley

Clearways
Industrial
Estate

Works

Church Road

Chancel
Close

Southfields

**WES
KIN**

163

556

Rushetts Road

Kn Cl

Brs

A   **B**   **C**   est Kingsdown
Industrial Estate   Ash Tree Drive   **D**

57

Kingsfield R

High
Castle
Wood

West Kingsdown
Medical Centre

1 grid square represents 500 metres

eedgate Hill

Michaels

Lane

itchers

E   Hill   Sun   Valley Rd   F   44   G   H

59   60

PH   PO   Small
Grains

**Fawkham
Green**

West Yoke

Ayelands

Tye   Ash Rd

Coltstead

Brands Hatch Road

Fawkham   Green   Road

Beechcroft Farm
Industrial Estate

1

Ash   Road

Red

2

Hotel

Rogers   Wood   Lane   Billet   Hill

65

Crowhurst Lane

The   Street

Ash

3

52

64

4

Kingsdown
House

South Ash Road

Wise's Lane

5

The London
Golf Club

Crowhurst

Golf Course

59   60

63

E   F   G   H

Ash Lane

Wise's
Lane

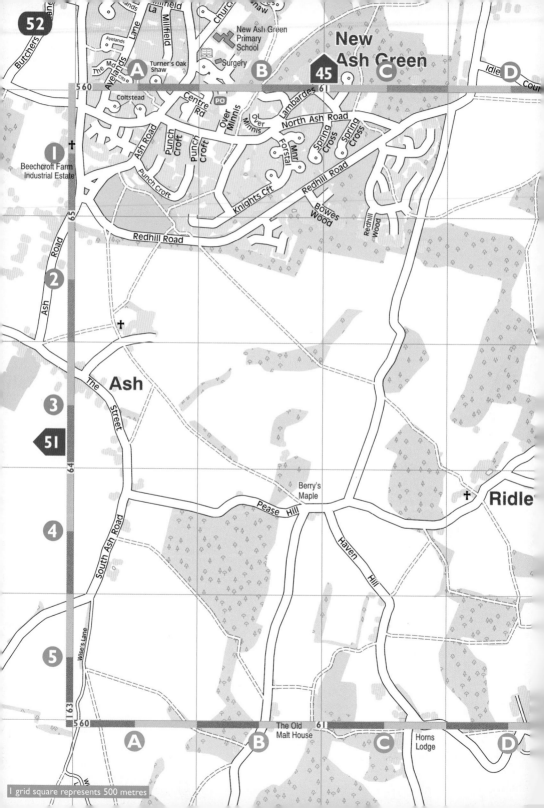

Ash	52 A3	Grays	7 G2
Barnehurst	2 B5	Greenhithe	15 F2
Barnes Cray	12 B1	Green Street Green	24 A5
Bean	24 B2	Grubb Street	34 B2
Betsham	25 F3	Hartley	45 F1
Bexleyheath	10 B1	Hartley Green	45 E1
Biggin	9 G1	Hawley	22 A4
Bowmans	11 H4	Heath Side	20 D1
Camer	47 G2	Henhurst	38 A2
Chalk	19 G5	Hextable	31 E1
Clement Street	21 H5	Hook Green	20 D3
Cobham	38 B5	Hook Green	25 F5
Coldblow	20 A1	Hook Green	47 E2
Crayford	12 A2	Horton Kirby	33 F5
Crockenhill	40 B3	Hulberry	41 F5
Darenth	23 E4	Istead Rise	36 C1
Dartford	12 C4	Joyden's Wood	20 D3
Dean Bottom	34 B4	Kings Farm	27 G2
Denton	19 E4	Knockhall	15 F2
Eynsford	42 A5	Lane End	23 F4
Farningham	42 C3	Longfield	35 F4
Fawkham Green	51 F1	Longfield Hill	36 B5
Fleet Downs	22 D1	Maplescombe	49 H3
Foxendown	47 G5	Maypole	11 G5
Gravesend	18 B2	Meopham	46 D5
Meopham Station	47 F1	Slade Green	
Milton	18 D3	Sole Street	
Nash Street	37 E3	South Darenth	
New Ash Green	45 G5	Southfleet	
New Barn	35 H3	South Street	
New House	26 C1	Speed Gate	
New Street	53 F3	Stone	
New Town	13 F3	Stonehill Green	
North End	2 D3	Stonewood	
Northfleet	17 E2	Sutton at Hone	
Northfleet Green	26 A4	Swanley	
Northumberland Heath	2 A2	Swanley Village	
Old Bexley	10 C4	Swanscombe	
Parrock Farm	27 H2	Temple Hill	
Perry Street	17 H4	Thong	
Pettings	52 D5	Tilbury	
Puddledock	20 B5	West Court	
Purfleet	4 C1	Wested Fm	
Ridley	52 D4	West Kingsdown	
Riverview Park	28 C3	Westwood	
Rosherville	17 H2	West Yoke	
Round Street	37 H5	White Oak	
Shorne	29 G4	Wilmington	
Shorne Ridgeway	39 F1		
Singlewell	27 G5		

USING THE STREET INDEX

Street names are listed alphabetically. Each street name is followed by its postal town or area locality, the Postcode District, the page number, and the reference to the square in which the name is found.

Standard index entries are shown as follows:

Abbey Rd *BXLYHS* DA6 ....**10** A1

Street names and selected addresses not shown on the map due to scale restrictions are shown in the index with an asterisk:

Abbey Pl *DART* * DA1......................**12** D2

GENERAL ABBREVIATIONS

ACC	ACCESS	E	EAST	LDG	LODGE	R	
ALY	ALLEY	EMB	EMBANKMENT	LGT	LIGHT	RBT	ROUNDA
AP	APPROACH	EMBY	EMBASSY	LK	LOCK	RD	
AR	ARCADE	ESP	ESPLANADE	LKS	LAKES	RDG	
ASS	ASSOCIATION	EST	ESTATE	LNDG	LANDING	REP	REP
AV	AVENUE	EX	EXCHANGE	LTL	LITTLE	RES	RESEF
BCH	BEACH	EXPY	EXPRESSWAY	LWR	LOWER	RFC	RUGBY FOOTBALL
BLDS	BUILDINGS	EXT	EXTENSION	MAG	MAGISTRATE	RI	
BND	BEND	F/O	FLYOVER	MAN	MANSIONS	RP	
BNK	BANK	FC	FOOTBALL CLUB	MD	MEAD	RW	
BR	BRIDGE	FK	FORK	MDW	MEADOWS	S	S
BRK	BROOK	FLD	FIELD	MEM	MEMORIAL	SCH	SC
BTM	BOTTOM	FLDS	FIELDS	MKT	MARKET	SE	SOUTH
BUS	BUSINESS	FLS	FALLS	MKTS	MARKETS	SER	SERVICE
BVD	BOULEVARD	FLS	FLATS	ML	MALL	SH	S
BY	BYPASS	FM	FARM	ML	MILL	SHOP	SHOI
CATH	CATHEDRAL	FT	FORT	MNR	MANOR	SKWY	SK
CEM	CEMETERY	FWY	FREEWAY	MS	MEWS	SMT	SL
CEN	CENTRE	FY	FERRY	MSN	MISSION	SOC	SC
CFT	CROFT	GA	GATE	MT	MOUNT	SP	
CH	CHURCH	GAL	GALLERY	MTN	MOUNTAIN	SPR	S
CHA	CHASE	GDN	GARDEN	MTS	MOUNTAINS	SQ	SC
CHYD	CHURCHYARD	GDNS	GARDENS	MUS	MUSEUM	ST	S
CIR	CIRCLE	GLD	GLADE	MWY	MOTORWAY	STN	S
CIRC	CIRCUS	GLN	GLEN	N	NORTH	STR	S
CL	CLOSE	GN	GREEN	NE	NORTH EAST	STRD	S
CLFS	CLIFFS	GND	GROUND	NW	NORTH WEST	SW	SOUTH
CMP	CAMP	GRA	GRANGE	O/P	OVERPASS	TDG	TR
CNR	CORNER	GRG	GARAGE	OFF	OFFICE	TER	TE
CO	COUNTY	GT	GREAT	ORCH	ORCHARD	THWY	THROUG
COLL	COLLEGE	GTWY	GATEWAY	OV	OVAL	TNL	T
COM	COMMON	GV	GROVE	PAL	PALACE	TOLL	TC
COMM	COMMISSION	HGR	HIGHER	PAS	PASSAGE	TPK	TUF
CON	CONVENT	HL	HILL	PAV	PAVILION	TR	
COT	COTTAGE	HLS	HILLS	PDE	PARADE	TRL	
COTS	COTTAGES	HO	HOUSE	PH	PUBLIC HOUSE	TWR	
CP	CAPE	HOL	HOLLOW	PK	PARK	U/P	UNDE
CPS	COPSE	HOSP	HOSPITAL	PKWY	PARKWAY	UNI	UNIV
CR	CREEK	HRB	HARBOUR	PL	PLACE	UPR	
CREM	CREMATORIUM	HTH	HEATH	PLN	PLAIN	V	
CRS	CRESCENT	HTS	HEIGHTS	PLNS	PLAINS	VA	
CSWY	CAUSEWAY	HVN	HAVEN	PLZ	PLAZA	VIAD	VI
CT	COURT	HWY	HIGHWAY	POL	POLICE STATION	VIL	
CTRL	CENTRAL	IMP	IMPERIAL	PR	PRINCE	VIS	
CTS	COURTS	IN	INLET	PREC	PRECINCT	VLG	V
CTYD	COURTYARD	IND EST	INDUSTRIAL ESTATE	PREP	PREPARATORY	VLS	
CUTT	CUTTINGS	INF	INFIRMARY	PRIM	PRIMARY	VW	
CV	COVE	INFO	INFORMATION	PROM	PROMENADE	W	
CYN	CANYON	INT	INTERCHANGE	PRS	PRINCESS	WD	
DEPT	DEPARTMENT	IS	ISLAND	PRT	PORT	WHF	
DL	DALE	JCT	JUNCTION	PT	POINT	WK	
DM	DAM	JTY	JETTY	PTH	PATH	WKS	
DR	DRIVE	KG	KING	PZ	PIAZZA	WLS	
DRO	DROVE	KNL	KNOLL	QD	QUADRANT	WY	
DRY	DRIVEWAY	L	LAKE	QU	QUEEN	YD	
DWGS	DWELLINGS	LA	LANE	QY	QUAY	YHA	YOUTH

OSTCODE TOWNS AND AREA ABBREVIATIONS

WK ....Borough Green/ West Kingsdown
....Bexley
N........................Bexleyheath north
S........................Bexleyheath south
CHF........................Chadwell St Mary/ Chafford Hundred

DART ....Dartford
ERITH ....Erith
EYN ....Eynsford
GRAYS ....Grays
GRH ....Greenhithe
GVE ....Gravesend east
GVW ....Gravesend west

HART ....Hartley
MEO ....Meopham
ORP ....Orpington
PUR ....Purfleet
RDART ....Rural Dartford
RSEV ....Rural Sevenoaks
STMC/STPC ......St Mary Cray/St Paul's Cray

STRD ....Strood
SWCM ....Swanscombe
SWLY ....Swanley
TIL ....Tilbury
WTHK ....West Thurrock

Index - streets

Abb - Bri

A

PI *DART* * DA1 ....12 D2
Rd *BXLYHS* DA6 ....10 A1
DA9 ....15 G2
DA12 ....19 E5
ts CI *SWLY* BR8 ....31 E5
Rd *DART* DA1 ....14 C3
DA9 ....14 C3
Rd *DART* DA1 ....11 H2
th PI *DART* * DA1 ....12 C3
de Rd *TIL* RM18 ....8 D3
als Wk *GRH* DA9 ....15 F2
e CI *GVE* DA12 ....27 F2
le CI *RDART* DA2 ....14 A3
n Gdns *RDART* DA2 ....14 B4
n Rd *SWCM* DA10 ....15 H3
ooke *GVE* DA12 ....18 C4
DART DA1 ....12 C1
Crs *EYN* DA4 ....42 C4
r Rd *TIL* RM18 ....9 E3
a Rd *BXLYHN* DA7 ....2 A3
Murray CI *GVE* DA12 .....18 C4
Rd *BXLY* DA5 ....10 C3
RT DA2 ....21 G2
M DA10 ....13 F3
Rd *BXLYHS* DA6 ....10 B1
DA12 ....18 C3
Ter *GVE* DA12 ....18 C3
ey Rd *ERITH* DA8 ....3 E2
y *SWLY* BR8 ....30 D3
der Rd *GRH* DA9 ....15 G2
dra CI *SWLY* BR8 ....30 C3
dra Rd *DART* DA1 ....18 B3
DA12 ....19 E4
M18 ....9 G3
dra Wk *EYN* * DA4 ....33 F3
PI *GVW* DA11 ....17 H5
Rd *GVW* DA11 ....27 F1
"T DA2 ....22 B3
st *GRAYS* RM17 ....8 A1
en La *GRH* DA9 ....15 G3
le CI *RDART* DA2 ....14 B5
ts CI *SWCM* DA10 ....16 B2
ts' Rd *GVW* DA11 ....17 H5
d *SWCM* DA10 ....16 A2
na *GVE* * DA12 ....28 B3
l Dr *SWLY* BR8 ....30 B4
r Rd *RDART* DA2 ....14 A4
t *BXLY* DA5 ....10 A5
re CI *DART* DA1 ....11 H1
d *SWCM* DA10 ....16 A3
Bvd *DART* * DA1 ....13 H3
DA9 ....14 A1
* CI *DART* DA1 ....11 F2
d *WTHK* RM20 ....6 D1
na PI *GVE* DA12 ....18 B3
Cleves Rd *DART* DA1 ....12 D2
ys La *SWLY* BR8 ....31 E2
d Rd *ERITH* DA8 ....2 D1
re Av *BXLYHN* DA7 ....2 A3
arth Dr *DART* DA1 ....22 A1
rch *SWLY* BR8 ....30 B5
aw CI *GVW* DA11 ....27 E4
n Dr *RDART* DA2 ....21 F2
St *ERITH* DA8 ....2 D1
ot La *BXLY* DA5 ....10 A3
n Av *BXLY* DA5 ....10 A3
CI *BXLY* DA5 ....10 A3
n Rd *BXLY* DA5 ....10 A4
Rd *MEO* DA13 ....36 C3
vy *SWLY* BR8 ....30 D3
a PI *GVE* * DA12 ....15 F1
st *GRAYS* RM17 ....7 H2
RM20 ....7 E1
GRH DA9 ....15 E2
GVE DA12 ....28 B3
nt Rd *TIL* RM18 ....9 E4
e *GVE* DA12 ....18 C4
v *MEO* DA13 ....47 F5
l *TIL* RM18 ....9 G3

Arnold Rd *GVE* DA12 ....27 G1
Arnolds La *RDART* DA2 ....22 C5
Arnsberg Wy *BXLYHN* DA7 ....10 C1
Arran CI *ERITH* DA8 ....2 B1
Artemis CI *GVE* DA12 ....19 E4
Arthur St *ERITH* DA8 ....2 D2
   GRAYS RM17 ....8 A1
   GVW DA11 ....18 A4
Artillery Rw *GVE* DA12 ....18 C4
Arundel CI *BXLY* DA5 ....10 B3
Arundel Rd *DART* DA1 ....12 C1
Ascot Rd *GVW* DA11 ....27 F2
Ash CI *SWLY* BR8 ....30 A3
Ashdown CI *BXLY* DA5 ....11 E4
Ashen Dr *DART* DA1 ....12 A3
Ashmore Gdns *GVW* DA11 ....26 B3
Ash Rd *BGR/WK* TN15 ....51 H2
   DART DA1 ....12 D5
   GVE DA12 ....27 G3
   HART DA3 ....35 E4
   HART DA3 ....52 A1
   RDART DA2 ....22 B3
Ashurst CI *DART* DA1 ....2 D5
Ashworth Av *BGR/WK* * TN15 ....50 C5
Aspdin Rd *GVW* DA11 ....26 B2
Aspen CI *SWLY* BR8 ....30 B2
Astley *GRAYS* RM17 ....7 F1
Astor Rd *BGR/WK* TN15 ....50 C4
Astra Dr *GVE* DA12 ....28 A4
Atlantic CI *SWCM* DA10 ....16 A2
Atlas Rd *DART* DA1 ....4 B5
Attlee Dr *DART* DA1 ....13 G2
Auckland CI *TIL* RM18 ....9 E4
Augustine Rd *GVE* DA12 ....18 C4
Austen CI *GRH* * DA9 ....15 C3
   TIL RM18 ....9 G4
Austin Rd *GVW* DA11 ....17 H5
Aveley CI *ERITH* DA8 ....2 D1
Avenue Rd *ERITH* DA8 ....2 A1
The Avenue *GVW* DA11 ....18 A5
Avon CI *GVE* DA12 ....27 H1
Avonmouth Rd *DART* DA1 ....12 D2
Axtane *MEO* * DA13 ....35 F1
Axtane CI *EYN* DA4 ....33 E3
Ayelands *HART* DA3 ....45 E5
Ayelands La *HART* DA3 ....52 A1
Azalea Dr *SWLY* BR8 ....30 B5

B

Back La *BXLY* DA5 ....10 C4
Bader Wk *GVW* DA11 ....26 C2
Badlow CI *ERITH* DA8 ....2 C3
Baker Hill CI *GVW* DA11 ....26 D3
Bakers Av *BGR/WK* TN15 ....50 C5
Baldwyn's Pk *BXLY* DA5 ....20 B1
Baldwyn's Rd *BXLY* DA5 ....20 B1
Balmoral Gdns *BXLY* DA5 ....10 B4
Balmoral Rd *EYN* DA4 ....32 C1
Banbury Vls *MEO* DA13 ....25 F5
Banckside *HART* DA3 ....35 E5
Bankside *GVW* DA11 ....17 E3
Bankside CI *RDART* DA2 ....20 B3
Banks La *BXLYHS* DA6 ....10 B1
Bank St *GVE* DA12 ....18 B3
Barfield *EYN* DA4 ....32 D2
Barham CI *GVE* DA12 ....19 F5
Barham Rd *DART* DA1 ....12 A1
Barnehurst Av *BXLYHN* DA7 ....2 A3
Barnehurst CI *ERITH* DA8 ....2 A3
Barnehurst Rd *BXLYHN* DA7 ....2 A4
Barn End Dr *RDART* DA2 ....21 G3
Barn End La *SWLY* BR8 ....21 G5
Barnes Cray Rd *DART* DA1 ....12 A1
Barnett CI *ERITH* DA8 ....2 A3
Barnfield *GVW* DA11 ....27 E1
Barnfield CI *GRH* DA9 ....14 D3
   HART DA3 ....36 B4
   SWLY BR8 ....40 A3
Barnwell Rd *DART* DA1 ....4 B5
Barrack Rw *GVW* * DA11 ....18 A3

Barr Rd *GVE* DA12 ....28 B1
Bartholomew Wy *SWLY* BR8 .....30 C4
Bartlett Rd *GVW* DA11 ....18 A5
Barton CI *BXLYHS* DA6 ....10 A2
Barton Rd *EYN* DA4 ....32 D2
Basing Dr *BXLY* DA5 ....10 B3
Bath Rd *DART* DA1 ....12 B4
Bath St *GVW* DA11 ....18 B3
Battle St *GVE* DA12 ....38 B4
Bayly Rd *DART* DA1 ....13 G3
Bay Manor La *WTHK* RM20 ....5 H1
Baynham CI *BXLY* DA5 ....10 B3
Bazes Shaw *HART* DA3 ....45 F5
Beacon Dr *RDART* DA2 ....24 C2
Beacon Rd *ERITH* DA8 ....3 F2
Beaconsfield Rd *BXLY* DA5 ....20 C1
Bean La *RDART* DA2 ....24 A1
Bean Rd *GRH* DA9 ....15 F3
Beaton CI *GRH* DA9 ....15 F1
Beatrice Gdns *GVW* DA11 ....26 C1
Beaumont Dr *GVW* DA11 ....17 G4
Beaumont Rd *GVW* DA11 ....17 G4
Beckley CI *GVE* DA12 ....28 D1
Bedford Rd *DART* DA1 ....13 G4
   GVW DA11 ....26 D1
Beech Av *SWLY* BR8 ....30 D5
Beechcroft Av *BXLYHN* DA7 ....2 B3
Beechenlea La *SWLY* BR8 ....31 E5
The Beeches *MEO* DA13 ....37 H5
   SWLY BR8 ....30 D1
   TIL RM18 ....9 F4
Beechfield Rd *ERITH* DA8 ....2 C2
Beechlands CI *HART* DA3 ....45 G1
Beech Rd *DART* DA1 ....12 D5
Beech Wk *DART* DA1 ....12 A1
Beesfield La *EYN* DA4 ....42 C4
Bell CI *GRH* DA9 ....14 D2
Bellevue Rd *BXLYHS* DA6 ....10 B2
Bellman Av *GVE* DA12 ....19 E5
Beltana Dr *GVE* DA12 ....28 A3
Belvedere CI *GVE* DA12 ....18 C5
Bennett Wy *RDART* DA2 ....23 F3
Benson Rd *GRAYS* RM17 ....7 H1
Bentley CI *HART* DA3 ....36 A4
Bentley St *GVE* DA12 ....18 C3
Beresford Rd *GVW* DA11 ....17 G4
Berkeley Crs *DART* DA1 ....13 F5
Berkeley Rd *GVE* DA12 ....18 B3
Berkley Rd *DART* DA1 ....18 B3
Berkley Rw *GVE* * DA12 ....18 B3
Bermuda Rd *TIL* RM18 ....9 E4
Bernard St *GVE* DA12 ....18 B3
Berrylands *HART* DA3 ....45 G2
Best Ter *SWLY* * BR8 ....40 A1
Betsham Rd *ERITH* DA8 ....2 D2
   MEO DA13 ....24 D4
   SWCM DA10 ....16 A4
Beult Rd *DART* DA1 ....3 E5
Bevan PI *SWLY* BR8 ....30 D5
Bevans CI *GRH* DA9 ....15 C3
Beverley Rd *BXLYHN* DA7 ....2 A4
Bevis CI *RDART* DA2 ....14 A4
Bexhill Dr *GRAYS* RM17 ....7 E1
Bexley CI *DART* DA1 ....11 G2
Bexley High St *BXLY* DA5 ....10 C4
Bexley La *DART* DA1 ....11 G2
Bexley Rd *ERITH* DA8 ....2 A2
Biddenden Wy *MEO* DA13 ....36 C2
Biggin La *GRAYS* RM17 ....9 F1
Billet HI *BGR/WK* TN15 ....51 G2
Billings *HART* DA3 ....45 F2
Bilton Rd *ERITH* DA8 ....3 E2
Birch CI *EYN* DA4 ....48 D1
   HART DA3 ....36 A3
The Birches *SWLY* BR8 ....30 C3
Birch PI *GRH* DA9 ....14 C3
Birchwood Dr *RDART* DA2 ....20 C3
Birchwood Park Av *SWLY* BR8 ...30 C4
Birchwood Rd *RDART* DA2 ....30 A1
Birchwood Ter *SWLY* * BR8 ....30 A2
Birling Rd *ERITH* DA8 ....3 F1
Birtrick Dr *MEO* DA13 ....46 D1
Bishops Ct *GRH* DA9 ....14 C2

Blackmans CI *DART* DA1 ....12 C5
Blake Gdns *DART* DA1 ....13 F1
Blenheim CI *DART* DA1 ....12 C3
   MEO DA13 ....47 E5
Blenheim Gv *GVE* DA12 ....18 C4
Blenheim Rd *DART* DA1 ....12 C3
Bligh Rd *GVW* DA11 ....18 A3
Blockhouse Rd *RDART* RM17 ......8 A1
Bodle Av *SWCM* DA10 ....16 A3
Boleyn Wy *SWCM* DA10 ....16 A4
Bonaventure Ct *GVE* DA12 ....28 B3
Bond St *GRAYS* RM17 ....8 A1
Bonney Wy *SWLY* BR8 ....30 C3
Borland CI *GRH* DA9 ....15 E2
Botsom La *BGR/WK* TN15 ....50 A4
Bott Rd *RDART* DA2 ....22 B3
Boucher Dr *GVW* DA11 ....26 D2
Boundary St *ERITH* DA8 ....2 D2
Bourne Md *BXLY* DA5 ....11 E2
Bourne Pde *BXLY* * DA5 ....10 D4
Bourne Rd *BXLY* DA5 ....10 D3
   GVE DA12 ....28 B1
Bourne Wy *SWLY* BR8 ....30 A4
Bow Arrow La *DART* DA1 ....13 G3
Bower La *EYN* DA4 ....49 E1
Bower Rd *SWLY* BR8 ....31 E1
Bowers Av *GVW* DA11 ....26 D3
Bowesden La *GVE* DA12 ....39 H1
Bowes Wd *HART* DA3 ....52 B1
Bowmans Rd *DART* DA1 ....11 H4
Bown CI *TIL* RM18 ....9 F4
Brackendene *BXLY* DA5 ....20 C3
Brackondale Av *MEO* DA13 ....36 D2
Bradbourne Rd *BXLY* DA5 ....10 C4
   GRAYS RM17 ....7 H1
Braemar Av *BXLYHN* DA7 ....11 E1
Braeside Crs *BXLYHN* DA7 ....11 E1
Brakefield Rd *MEO* DA13 ....25 H5
Brakes PI *BGR/WK* TN15 ....50 C4
Bramble Av *RDART* DA2 ....24 C2
Brambledown *HART* DA3 ....35 F5
Bramblefield CI *HART* DA3 ....34 D4
Bramley CI *MEO* DA13 ....36 D1
   SWLY BR8 ....30 C5
Bramley PI *DART* DA1 ....12 A1
Brandon Rd *DART* DA1 ....13 G4
Brandon St *GVW* DA11 ....18 B4
Brands Hatch Pk *HART* * DA3 ....50 D1
Brands Hatch Rd *BGR/WK* TN15 .51 E1
Bransell CI *SWLY* BR8 ....40 A2
Branton Rd *GRH* DA9 ....14 D3
Brantwood Av *ERITH* DA8 ....2 A2
Brasted Rd *ERITH* DA8 ....2 C2
Breach Rd *WTHK* RM20 ....5 H1
Breakneck HI *GRH* DA9 ....15 F2
Bremner CI *SWLY* BR8 ....31 E5
Brenchley Av *GVW* DA11 ....27 F4
Brendon CI *BXLYHN* DA7 ....2 C3
Brennan Rd *TIL* RM18 ....9 F4
Brent CI *BXLY* DA5 ....10 A5
   RDART DA2 ....13 H3
Brentfield Rd *DART* DA1 ....13 G3
Brentlands Dr *DART* DA1 ....13 G5
Brent La *DART* DA1 ....13 H4
The Brent *DART* DA1 ....13 H4
Brent Wy *DART* DA1 ....13 H3
Brewers Fld *RDART* DA2 ....21 G3
Brewers Rd *GVE* DA12 ....39 E2
Brewhouse Yd *GVE* DA12 ....18 B3
Briar Rd *BXLY* DA5 ....20 B2
The Briars *BGR/WK* TN15 ....50 B4
Briars Wy *HART* DA3 ....45 G1
Brick Ct *GRAYS* * RM17 ....7 G1
Bridge CI *GRH* DA9 ....5 F5
Bridge Ct *GRAYS* * RM17 ....7 H1
Bridgen Rd *BXLY* DA5 ....10 A4
Bridge Rd *ERITH* DA8 ....2 D3
   GRAYS RM17 ....7 H1
Bridges Dr *DART* DA1 ....13 H2
Brightlands *DART* DA1 ....26 C3
Brimstone HI *MEO* DA13 ....47 G5
Bristol Rd *GVE* DA12 ....27 H2

Britannia Dr GVE DA12 ....28 B4
Broad Ditch Rd MEO DA13........36 A1
Broad La RDART DA2.................21 F3
Broadoak Cl RDART DA2.............22 C5
Broadoak Rd ERITH DA8..............2 B2
Broad Rd SWCM DA10...............16 A3
Broadway BXLYHS DA6...............10 A1
  GRAYS RM17.............................8 A1
  TIL RM18..................................8 D4
Broadwood GVW DA11...............27 F4
Bromley GRAYS RM17..................7 F1
Brompton Dr ERITH DA8...............3 F2
Bronte Cl TIL RM18......................9 G4
Bronte Gv DART DA1..................13 F1
Bronte Vw GVE DA12..................18 C5
Brookdale Rd BXLY DA5..............10 A3
Brooke Dr GVE DA12..................19 H5
Brooklands DART DA1.................13 E5
Brook Rd GVW DA11...................17 G5
  SWLY BR8..............................30 B4
Brookside Rd MEO DA13.............36 D1
Brook St ERITH DA8.....................2 A1
Broomfield Rd BXLYHS DA6.........10 C2
  SWCM DA10............................16 A3
Broomfields HART DA3...............45 E1
Broomhill Ri BXLYHS DA6............10 C2
Broomhill Rd DART DA1..............12 B3
Broom Md BXLYHS DA6...............10 C3
Broomwood Cl BXLY DA5.............20 B1
Browning Rd DART DA1..............13 F1
Brown Rd GVE DA12...................28 A1
Bruces Wharf Rd GRAYS RM17......7 G1
Brunel Cl TIL RM18......................9 F4
Brunswick Wk GVE DA12............18 D3
Bryanston Rd TIL RM18................9 G4
Buckingham Rd GVW DA11.........17 F4
Buckley Cl DART DA1....................2 D4
Bucks Cross Rd GVW DA11..........26 D2
Bullivant Cl GRH DA9.................15 E2
Bull Yd GVE * DA12....................28 B3
The Bungalows WTHK * RM20.......6 A1
Bunny Hl GVE * DA12.................29 G5
Burdett Av GVE DA12.................29 G3
Burgate Cl DART DA1...................2 D5
Burghfield Rd MEO DA13............36 D1
Burman Cl RDART DA2................14 A4
Burnaby Rd GVW DA11..............17 G4
Burnett Rd ERITH DA8..................3 H1
Burnham Crs DART DA1..............12 C1
Burnham Rd DART DA1...............12 D2
Burnham Ter DART * DA1............12 D2
Burnley Rd WTHK RM20................5 H3
Burns Cl ERITH DA8......................2 C3
Burns Pl TIL RM18........................9 F3
Burnt House La RDART DA2.........22 A3
Burr Bank Ter RDART * DA2.........21 G3
Butchers La BGR/WK TN15.........44 D5
Butlers Pl HART * DA3................52 A1
Butterfly Av DART DA1...............22 B1
Butterly Av DART * DA1..............22 B1
Button St SWLY BR8...................31 C5
Buxton Rd ERITH DA8...................2 B2
Bycliffe Ms GVW * DA11............17 H4
Bycliffe Ter GVW * DA11............17 H4
Byron Gdns TIL RM18...................9 G3
Byron Rd DART DA1....................13 H1

C

Cadogan Av RDART DA2.............14 B4
Cairns Cl DART DA1....................12 D2
Calcutta Rd TIL RM18...................8 D4
Calderwood GVE DA12...............28 A5
Calfstock La EYN DA4.................32 A5
Caling Cft HART DA3..................45 F4
Caliph Cl GVE DA12...................28 B2
Cambria Crs GVE DA12...............28 A3
Cambrian Gv GVW DA11............18 A4
Camden Cl GVW DA11................17 E5
Camden Rd BXLY DA5.................10 B5
Cameron Cl BXLY DA5................20 B2
Camer Park Rd MEO DA13..........47 F3
Camer Rd MEO DA13..................47 G2
Camer St MEO DA13...................47 G2
Campbell Rd GVW DA11.............17 H5
Campion Cl GVW DA11...............26 C3
Camrose Av ERITH * DA8.............2 A1
Canada Farm Rd EYN DA4...........44 B1
Canada Rd ERITH DA8..................3 F2
Canal Basin GVE DA12................18 D3
Canal Rd GVE DA12....................18 D3
Canberra Sq TIL * RM18...............9 E4
Canterbury Cl DART DA1.............13 G4
Canterbury Rd GVE DA12............27 G1
Canterbury Wy DART DA1...........14 A1
  WTHK RM20.............................5 G2

Capel Pl RDART DA2..................21 G3
Capstan Ct GRH DA9.................14 A1
Carleton Pl EYN DA4..................33 E5
Carleton Rd DART DA1...............13 G4
Carlisle Rd DART DA1.................13 G3
Carlton Av GRH DA9..................14 C3
Carlton Rd ERITH DA8..................2 A1
Carmelite Wy HART DA3............45 F1
Carrington Rd DART DA1............13 F3
Carsington Gdns DART DA1........21 H1
Carter Av BGR/WK * TN15..........50 C5
Casstine Cl SWLY BR8................30 D2
Castlefields MEO DA13...............36 D2
Castle Hl HART DA3...................44 D1
Castle La GVE DA12...................28 D1
Castle Rd EYN DA4....................48 B4
  GRAYS RM17.............................7 E1
  SWCM DA10............................16 B3
Castle St GRH DA9.....................15 E2
  SWCM DA10............................16 B3
Castleton Av BXLYHN DA7............2 B3
Cavell Crs DART DA1..................13 G1
Cavendish Av ERITH DA8.............2 A1
Cavendish Sq HART DA3............34 D4
Caxton Cl HART DA3..................35 F5
Cecil Rd GVW DA11...................17 H5
Cedar Av GVE DA12...................27 G3
Cedar Cl MEO DA13...................47 E2
  SWLY BR8..............................30 A3
Cedar Dr EYN DA4.....................32 D3
Cedar Rd DART DA1...................12 D5
  ERITH DA8................................3 E3
Celia Av BGR/WK * TN15...........50 C5
Central Av GVE DA12.................27 F1
  TIL RM18..................................8 E3
Central Rd DART DA1.................13 E2
Centre Rd HART DA3..................52 A1
Cerne Rd GVE DA12...................28 A3
Cervia Wy GVE DA12.................28 B2
Chadfields TIL RM18....................9 E3
Chadwick Cl GVW DA11.............26 C1
Chalet Cl RDART DA2.................20 B3
Chalice Wy GRH DA9.................14 C2
Chalk Ct GRAYS * RM17...............7 G1
Chalk Rd GVE DA12...................19 G5
Chalky Bank GVW DA11.............27 E3
Challenge Cl GVE DA12..............28 B3
Chambers Cl GRH DA9...............15 E2
Chancel Cl BGR/WK TN15..........50 C5
Chantry Av HART DA3................45 E2
Chapel Cl DART DA1...................11 G2
  WTHK RM20.............................6 B1
Chapel Hl DART DA1..................11 G1
Chapel Rd BXLYHN DA7..............10 C1
Chapel Wd HART DA3................45 E5
Chapel Wood Rd HART DA3........45 E5
Chapman's Hl BGR/WK TN15......53 G4
Charles St GRAYS RM17...............7 H1
  GRH DA9................................14 D2
Charlieville Rd ERITH DA8.............2 A2
Charlotte Cl BXLYHS DA6............10 A2
Charlotte Pl WTHK RM20..............6 B1
Charlton St WTHK RM20................6 D1
Charnock SWLY BR8...................30 C5
Charter Dr BXLY DA5..................10 A4
Chase Sq GVE * DA12.................18 B3
The Chase WTHK RM20................6 D1
Chastilian Rd DART DA1..............12 A4
Chatsworth Rd DART DA1............12 C1
Chaucer Cl TIL RM18....................9 G4
Chaucer Pk DART DA1................13 F4
Chaucer Rd GVW DA11...............26 B2
Chaucer Wy DART DA1...............13 G1
Chave Rd DART DA1...................22 A2
Cheltenham Cl GVE DA12............27 G4
The Chenies RDART DA2.............20 C3
Chequers Cl MEO DA13..............36 C3
Cherry Av SWLY BR8...................30 B4
Cherry Tree La RDART DA2..........20 D2
Cherry Trees HART DA3...............45 F2
Cherrywood Dr GVW DA11..........26 C3
Cheshunt Cl MEO DA13...............47 E2
Chesterfield Dr DART DA1............12 B2
Chestnut Av DART DA1................14 D4
Chestnut Cl GVW DA11...............17 H3
Chestnut Gv RDART DA2.............20 B4
Chestnut Rd DART DA1................12 D5
Cheswick Cl DART DA1................11 H1
Chesworth Cl ERITH DA8..............2 C3
Cheviot Rd BXLYHN DA7..............2 C4
Cheyne Wk DART DA1.................47 E5
Chichester Ri GVE DA12..............27 H3
Chichester Rd GVW DA11............14 D2
Chieveley Rd BXLYHN DA7..........10 D1
Chiffinch Gdns GVW DA11..........26 C2
Childs Crs SWCM DA10...............15 H3
Chilham Cl BXLY DA5.................10 B4
Chiltern Cl BXLYHN DA7...............2 C3

Chiltern Rd GVW DA11................26 C2
Chipstead Rd ERITH DA8..............2 C2
Christ Church Av ERITH DA8..........2 B1
Christ Church Rd GVE DA12.........18 C5
Christchurch Rd DART DA1...........12 C4
  TIL RM18..................................9 E3
Christian Fields Av GVE DA12.......27 G3
Church Aly GVE * DA12...............18 B3
Church Cl DART DA1...................21 H1
Church Fld DART DA1..................21 H1
Church Hl DART DA1...................11 C1
  DART DA1................................21 H2
  GRH DA9................................14 C2
Churchill Cl DART DA1.................13 H5
Churchill Rd EYN DA4.................33 E5
  GRAYS RM17.............................8 B1
  GVW DA11..............................17 H5
Church La GVE DA12...................29 E1
Church Pth GRH DA9..................14 D3
  GVW DA11..............................17 E3
Church Rd BGR/WK TN15...........50 C5
  EYN DA4.................................22 C5
  GRH DA9................................14 C2
  HART DA3...............................45 F1
  MEO DA13...............................37 G1
  SWCM DA10............................16 B3
  SWLY BR8..............................31 H2
  SWLY BR8..............................40 B3
  TIL RM18..................................8 C3
Church St GRAYS RM17.................8 A1
  GVW DA11..............................18 B3
  MEO DA13...............................25 G4
Church Wk DART DA1.................21 H2
  GVE DA12...............................18 D4
Cimba Wd GVE DA12..................28 A3
Cirrus Crs GVE DA12...................28 A4
Civic Sq TIL RM18.........................9 E4
Clare Cswy GRH DA9..................14 C1
Claremont Crs DART DA1.............11 G1
Claremont Rd SWLY BR8.............30 C1
Clarence Pl GVE DA12.................18 B4
Clarence Rd BXLYHS DA6............10 A1
  GRAYS RM17.............................7 G1
Clarence Rw GVE DA12...............18 B4
Clarendon Gdns RDART DA2........14 B5
Clarendon Pl RDART DA2.............20 B4
Clarendon Rd GVE DA12.............18 C3
Clarkbourne Dr GRAYS RM17........8 B1
Clark Cl ERITH DA8.......................3 E3
Claston Cl DART DA1...................11 G1
Clayton Croft Rd RDART DA2........21 E1
Claywood La RDART DA2.............24 D2
Clement St SWLY BR8.................21 H5
Cliff Reach GRH DA9..................14 C3
Clifton Gv GVW DA11.................18 B4
Clifton Marine Pde GVW DA11......17 H3
Clifton Rd GVW DA11.................18 A3
Clipper Bvd GRH DA9.................14 C1
Clipper Bvd West GRH DA9............5 F5
Clipper Crs GVE DA12.................28 B3
Clive Av DART DA1.....................11 H5
Clive Rd GVE DA12.....................18 D4
The Close BXLY DA5....................10 C3
  HART DA3...............................35 H3
  RDART DA2.............................21 G2
Cloudesley Rd ERITH DA8............26 C3
The Clovers GVW DA11...............26 C3
Clydon Cl ERITH DA8....................2 C1
Cob Dr GVE DA12.......................29 G4
Cobhambury Rd GVE DA12..........38 C5
Cobham St GVW DA11................18 A4
Cobham Ter GRH * DA9..............15 F2
  GVW * DA11............................17 H5
Codrington Crs GVE DA12............27 G4
Codrington Gdns GVE DA12.........27 H4
Cold Blow Crs BXLY DA5..............11 F5
Coldharbour Rd GVW DA11.........26 C1
Coleridge Rd DART DA1...............13 G1
Colin Chapman Wy HART DA3......50 D1
Colin Cl RDART DA2....................13 H3
College Rd GVW DA11.................16 D2
  SWLY BR8..............................30 C1
Coller Crs RDART DA2.................14 C4
Collington Cl GVW DA11.............17 G4
Colney Rd DART DA1..................13 F3
Coltsfoot Ct GRAYS RM17.............8 B1
Coltstead HART DA3...................45 E5
  HART DA3...............................52 A1
Columbia Wharf Rd GRAYS RM17...7 G1
Colyer Rd GVW DA11.................26 B1
Colyers Cl ERITH DA8...................2 B1
Colyers La ERITH DA8...................2 A3
Comfrey Ct GRAYS RM17.............8 B1
Commercial Pl GVE DA12............18 C3
Common La RDART DA2..............21 E1
Compton Pl ERITH DA8.................2 D1
Conifer Av HART DA3.................45 E2

Conifer Wy SWLY BR8.................
Coniston Cl BXLYHN DA7............
  DART DA1.............................
  ERITH DA8.............................
Coniston Rd BXLYHN DA7...........
Constable Rd GVW DA11............
Constitution Hl GVE DA12...........
Consul Gdns SWLY * BR8............
Conway Gdns GRAYS RM17.........
Coombe Rd GVE DA12................
Coombfield Dr RDART DA2...........
Cooper Cl GRH DA9....................
Coopers Cl EYN DA4...................
Cooper Shaw Rd TIL RM18..........
Cooper's Rd GVW DA11...............
Copper Beech Cl GVE DA12.........
Copperfield Cl GVE DA12.............
The Coppice BXLY DA5................
Copse Side HART DA3.................
Copt Hall Rd MEO DA13..............
Cornwallis Cl ERITH DA8.............
Cornwall Rd DART DA1...............
Cornwell Av GVE DA12...............
Cotswold Cl BXLYHN DA7............
Cotswold Rd GVW DA11..............
Cotton La GRH DA9....................
Coulton Av GVW DA11................
Council Av GVW DA11.................
Court Crs SWLY BR8...................
Court Rd RDART DA2..................
Coutts Av GVE DA12...................
Cowdrey Ct DART DA1................
Cowley Av GVW DA11.................
Cowper Av TIL RM18...................
Crandon Wk EYN * DA4...............
Cranford Rd DART DA1................
Cranleigh Cl BXLY * DA5..............
Cranleigh Dr SWLY BR8...............
Crawfords SWLY BR8...................
Crayburne MEO DA13..................
Cray Cl DART DA1......................
Craydene Rd ERITH DA8..............
Crayford High St DART DA1..........
Crayford Rd DART DA1................
Crayford Wy DART DA1...............
Craylands La SWCM DA10............
Craylands Sq SWCM DA10............
Cray Rd SWLY BR8.....................
Credo Wy WTHK RM20................
The Creek GVW DA11..................
Cremorne Rd DART DA1...............
Crescent Ct GRAYS * RM17..........
Crescent Gdns SWLY BR8............
Crescent Rd ERITH DA8...............
The Crescent GRH DA9................
  GVW DA11.............................
  HART DA3.............................
Crest Av GRAYS RM17.................
Crest Vw GRH DA9.....................
Crete Hall Rd GVW DA11.............
Crockenhall Wy MEO DA13...........
Crockenhill La SWLY BR8.............
The Croft SWLY BR8....................
Crooked La GVE DA12.................
Cross La BXLY DA5.....................
Cross La East GVE DA12..............
Cross La West GVW DA11.............
Cross Rd DART DA1....................
  GVW DA11.............................
  RDART DA2............................
Cross St ERITH DA8....................
Crossways Bvd GRH DA9.............
Crowhurst La BGR/WK TN15.........
Crown Gn GVE DA12...................
Crown La GVE DA12....................
Crown Rd GRAYS RM17...............
Cruden Rd GVE DA12..................
Cugley Rd RDART DA2................
Culcroft HART DA3.....................
Culvey Cl HART DA3...................
Cumberland Av GVE DA12...........
Cumberland Dr DART DA1............
Cumbrian Av BXLYHN DA7...........
The Curlews GVE DA12................
Curzon Dr GRAYS RM17..............
Cutmore St GVW DA11................
Cutty Sark Ct GRH * DA9.............
Cuxton Cl BXLYHS DA6................
Cyclamen Rd SWLY BR8..............

D

Dabbling Cl ERITH * DA8.............
Dahlia Dr SWLY BR8...................
Dairy Cl EYN DA4.......................
Dale Cl DART DA1......................

Rd DART DA1 ... 11 H3
) DA13 ... 25 G3
Y BR8 ... 30 A4
/w ERITH DA8 ... 3 E4
is Rd SWLY BR8 ... 40 A5
jos Rd GVE DA12 ... 19 F5
Cl BXLY DA5 ... 10 C4
s Cl GVW DA11 ... 26 A2
ith Dr GVE DA12 ... 19 H5
ith Hl RDART DA2 ... 22 D4
ith Park Av RDART DA2 ... 23 F1
ith Pl RDART * DA2 ... 23 F4
ith Rd DART DA1 ... 22 C1
ith Rd South RDART DA2 ... 22 D3
ith Wood Rd RDART DA2 ... 14 C5
t Md EYN DA4 ... 32 D2
t Valley Pth DART DA1 ... 3 H3
DA4 ... 42 D1
n Cl DART DA1 ... 2 D5
ey Rd GRAYS * RM17 ... 7 H1
/ DA11 ... 18 A3
ey St GVW DA11 ... 18 A4
Hl SWLY BR8 ... 40 A3
ord Rd BXLY DA5 ... 11 E5
T DA1 ... 12 A3
DA4 ... 42 B2
n Rd TIL RM18 ... 8 D3
vood Cl BXLYHS DA6 ... 10 C2
vood Rd GVW DA11 ... 18 A5
Av GVW DA11 ... 17 G5
s Pl GVE DA12 ... 28 A5
s Cl GRH DA9 ... 14 D2
on Dr SWLY BR8 ... 30 C1
n Dr ERITH DA8 ... 3 H1
bant Cl ERITH DA8 ... 2 B1
urst Cl HART DA3 ... 36 A4
ell BXLY DA5 ... 11 G5
Cl RDART DA2 ... 20 C3
Dr HART DA3 ... 35 H3
Holm Rd GVW DA11 ... 26 B2
Rd DART DA1 ... 13 F4
way MEO DA13 ... 47 E2
Wk HART DA3 ... 35 E4
s Rd GVW DA11 ... 27 E2
n Court Rd GVE DA12 ... 19 E5
n Rd BXLY DA5 ... 11 G5
n St GVE DA12 ... 19 E4
n Ter BXLY * DA5 ... 20 C1
n Whf GVE * DA12 ... 19 F3
r Rd DART DA1 ... 12 A4
Wy GVE DA12 ... 19 F5
nt Cl DART DA1 ... 12 B5
Rd ERITH DA8 ... 2 B2
DA11 ... 17 F5
Rd EYN DA4 ... 32 D2
shire Av DART DA1 ... 12 B3
shire Rd BXLYHS DA6 ... 10 A1
DA11 ... 18 B5
nds Av RDART DA2 ... 13 H4
GRH DA9 ... 15 G2
s Av DART DA1 ... 13 G1
M18 ... 9 F3
s Cl HART DA3 ... 45 E1
s Rd GVE DA12 ... 19 E5
n Rd GVE DA12 ... 28 A4
d GRAYS RM17 ... 8 B1
od Cl GVW DA11 ... 26 D3
s Cottages EYN * DA4 ... 32 D5
Biggs Dr GVE DA12 ... 18 C5
/ La EYN DA4 ... 42 D5
ster Cl DART DA1 ... 13 F4
ster Rd GVE DA12 ... 27 H2
/ BXLYHN DA7 ... 2 A3
rs Dr MEO DA13 ... 47 F3
y Evans Cl BXLYHN DA7 ... 10 D1
Crs GVE DA12 ... 28 A3
ddons Ct GRAYS RM17 ... 8 A1
le Rd RDART DA2 ... 14 A5
d GVW DA11 ... 17 F4
d East GVW DA11 ... 17 G4
wnage GVW DA11 ... 27 E1
ank Av BXLYHN DA7 ... 2 B3
Av DART DA1 ... 13 G4
Rd MEO DA13 ... 26 B3
Va HART DA3 ... 35 E5
view Cl SWLY BR8 ... 30 D4
ERITH DA8 ... 2 C3
ve GVE DA12 ... 27 H3
DA3 ... 35 H4
ve Wy MEO DA13 ... 36 C1
on Wy RDART DA2 ... 24 B2
ond Cl ERITH DA8 ... 2 C3
Pl TIL RM18 ... 9 F3
s Rd DART DA1 ... 11 H2
Rd GVW DA11 ... 17 G4
ry Rd DART DA1 ... 12 B3
rch BXLY DA5 ... 11 E5
Rd DART DA1 ... 13 G1

Dunkirk Cl GVE DA12 ... 27 G4
Dunlop Rd TIL RM18 ... 8 D3
Durant Rd SWLY BR8 ... 21 E5
Duriun Wy ERITH DA8 ... 3 F2
Durndale La GVW DA11 ... 26 C3
Durrant Wy SWCM DA10 ... 16 A4
Dykewood Cl BXLY DA5 ... 20 B2

E

Eagles Rd GRH DA9 ... 15 F1
Eagle Wy GVW DA11 ... 16 C2
Eardemont Cl DART DA1 ... 11 H1
Earl Rd GVW DA11 ... 26 C1
Eastern Wy GRAYS RM17 ... 7 G1
East Hl DART DA1 ... 13 F4
EYN DA4 ... 33 F2
East Hill Dr DART DA1 ... 13 F4
East Holme ERITH DA8 ... 2 B3
East Kent Av GVW DA11 ... 17 E3
Eastleigh Rd BXLYHN DA7 ... 2 A4
East Ml GVW DA11 ... 17 H3
East Milton Rd GVE DA12 ... 18 D4
East Rochester Wy DART DA1 ... 11 F4
East St BXLYHN DA7 ... 10 C1
WTHK RM20 ... 7 E1
East Ter GVE DA12 ... 18 C3
East Thurrock Rd GRAYS RM17 ... 7 H1
Echo Ct GVE DA12 ... 27 G1
Eden Cl BXLY DA5 ... 20 B3
Edendale Rd BXLYHN DA7 ... 2 B3
Eden Pl GVE DA12 ... 18 B4
Eden Rd BXLY DA5 ... 20 A3
Edgar Cl SWLY BR8 ... 30 D4
Edgefield Cl DART DA1 ... 13 H5
Edgehill Gdns MEO DA13 ... 36 D2
Edinburgh Ms TIL RM18 ... 9 F4
Ediva Rd MEO DA13 ... 47 E1
Edmund Cl MEO DA13 ... 47 E1
Edwards Ct EYN DA4 ... 49 E1
Edwards Gdns SWLY BR8 ... 30 B5
Edwin Petty Pl RDART * DA2 ... 14 A4
Edwin Rd RDART DA2 ... 21 F2
Edwin St GVE DA12 ... 18 B4
Egerton Av SWLY BR8 ... 30 D2
Egerton Cl DART DA1 ... 12 B5
Eglantine La EYN DA4 ... 42 D2
Eglinton Rd SWCM DA10 ... 16 B3
Elgar Gdns TIL RM18 ... 9 E3
Eliot Rd DART DA1 ... 13 H2
Elizabeth Cl TIL RM18 ... 9 F4
Elizabeth Huggins Cottages
GVW * DA11 ... 27 F1
Elizabeth Pl EYN * DA4 ... 42 B2
Elizabeth St GRH DA9 ... 14 C2
Ellerman Rd TIL RM18 ... 8 D4
Elliott St GVE DA12 ... 18 D4
Ellis Waterton Cl SWLY BR8 ... 30 B5
Ellis Wy DART * DA1 ... 22 B1
Elm Cl DART DA1 ... 12 C5
Elm Dr SWLY BR8 ... 30 B3
Elmfield Cl GVW DA11 ... 18 B5
Elm Gv ERITH DA8 ... 2 B2
Elmington Cl BXLY DA5 ... 10 D4
Elm Rd DART DA1 ... 12 D5
ERITH DA8 ... 3 E3
GRAYS RM17 ... 8 A1
GRH DA9 ... 14 C3
GVE DA12 ... 27 G2
Elmstead Rd ERITH DA8 ... 2 C3
Elm Ter WTHK RM20 ... 6 B1
Elmwood Dr BXLY DA5 ... 10 A4
Elrick Cl ERITH DA8 ... 2 C1
Elwill Wy MEO DA13 ... 36 D2
Ely Cl ERITH DA8 ... 2 D4
Emersons Av SWLY BR8 ... 30 D1
Emerton Cl BXLYHS DA6 ... 10 A1
Emes Rd ERITH DA8 ... 2 A2
Empress Rd GVE DA12 ... 19 E4
Erith High St ERITH DA8 ... 2 D1
Esher Cl BXLY DA5 ... 10 A5
Eskdale Cl RDART DA2 ... 23 E1
Essex Rd DART * DA1 ... 12 D3
GVW DA11 ... 18 A5
HART DA3 ... 34 D3
WTHK RM20 ... 6 A1
Ethelbert Rd ERITH DA8 ... 2 A2
Ethelbery Rd RDART DA2 ... 22 A3
Eton Wy DART DA1 ... 12 C1
Europa Pk WTHK * RM20 ... 6 C1
Evans Cl GRH DA9 ... 15 E2
Evenden Rd MEO DA13 ... 47 E3
Everest Cl GVW DA11 ... 26 C2
Everest Pl SWLY BR8 ... 30 B5
Everglade Cl HART DA3 ... 35 F5
Eversley Av BXLYHN DA7 ... 2 C4
Eversley Cross BXLYHN DA7 ... 2 C4
Evesham Rd GVE DA12 ... 27 H1
Exeter Rd GVE DA12 ... 27 H2
Exmouth Rd GRAYS RM17 ... 7 H1
Eynsford Ri EYN DA4 ... 48 D2
Eynsford Rd EYN DA4 ... 42 B4
GRH DA9 ... 15 G2
SWLY BR8 ... 40 C2

F

Factory Rd GVW DA11 ... 17 E3
Faesten Wy BXLY DA5 ... 20 C2
Fairby Hl HART * DA3 ... 45 E1
Fairby La HART DA3 ... 45 E2
Fairfax Rd TIL RM18 ... 8 D3
Fairfield GVE DA12 ... 28 A4
Fairford Av BXLYHN DA7 ... 2 A3
Fairlight Cross HART DA3 ... 35 H4
Fairview ERITH DA8 ... 2 D2
HART * DA3 ... 51 F1
Fairview Gdns MEO DA13 ... 47 F1
Fairview Rd MEO DA13 ... 36 B1
Fairway BXLYHS DA6 ... 10 A2
Fairway Dr RDART DA2 ... 13 H4
The Fairway GVW DA11 ... 27 E1
Falcon Av GRAYS RM17 ... 7 H2
Falcon Cl DART DA1 ... 13 F2
Falcon Ms GVW DA11 ... 17 G5
Fallowfield RDART DA2 ... 24 B2
Farley Rd GVE DA12 ... 19 F4
Farlow Cl GVW DA11 ... 26 D2
Farm Av SWLY BR8 ... 30 A4
Farmcroft GVW DA11 ... 27 E1
Farm Holt HART DA3 ... 45 F4
Farm La WTHK RM20 ... 7 E1
Farm Pl DART DA1 ... 12 A1
Farm V BXLY DA5 ... 10 D3
Farningham Hill Rd SWLY BR8 ... 41 G1
Farnol Rd DART DA1 ... 13 G1
Farriers Cl GVE DA12 ... 19 F5
Fawkes Av DART DA1 ... 22 B1
Fawkham Av HART DA3 ... 36 A4
Fawkham Green Rd HART DA3 ... 51 F1
Fawkham Rd BGR/WK TN15 ... 50 D2
HART DA3 ... 34 D5
Faygate Crs BXLYHS DA6 ... 10 C2
Feenan Hwy TIL RM18 ... 9 F2
Fens Wy SWLY BR8 ... 21 E5
Ferguson Av GVE DA12 ... 27 G3
Fernbank EYN * DA4 ... 42 B5
Fern Cl ERITH DA8 ... 3 F3
Ferndale Rd GVE DA12 ... 27 F1
Ferndell Av BXLY DA5 ... 20 B2
Ferndene HART DA3 ... 36 B4
Fernheath Wy RDART DA2 ... 20 B4
Ferry Rd TIL RM18 ... 9 E4
Festival Av HART DA3 ... 36 B4
Festival Cl ERITH DA8 ... 2 D2
Fiddlers Cl GRH DA9 ... 15 F1
Fielding Av TIL RM18 ... 9 F3
Field Rd BGR/WK TN15 ... 53 G3
MEO DA13 ... 53 H2
Fifth Av WTHK RM20 ... 6 A1
Filborough Wy GVE DA12 ... 19 H5
Finchley Cl DART DA1 ... 13 G3
Finchley Rd GRAYS RM17 ... 7 H1
Finsbury Wy BXLY DA5 ... 10 B3
Firecrest Cl HART DA3 ... 35 H4
Firmin Rd DART DA1 ... 12 C2
First Av GVW DA11 ... 17 G5
WTHK RM20 ... 6 A1
The Firs BXLY DA5 ... 11 F5
Fishermen's Hl GVW DA11 ... 16 D2
Fiveash Rd GVW DA11 ... 17 H4
Five Wents SWLY BR8 ... 31 E3
Fleet Av RDART DA2 ... 14 A5
Fleetdale Pde RDART * DA2 ... 14 A5
Fleet Rd GVW DA11 ... 26 A2
RDART DA2 ... 14 A5
Fleming Gdns TIL RM18 ... 9 G3
Flint St WTHK RM20 ... 6 B1
Florence Cl WTHK RM20 ... 7 E1
Flowerhill Wy MEO DA13 ... 36 C1
Foord Cl RDART DA2 ... 23 G1
Ford Rd GVW DA11 ... 16 D2
Foresters Crs BXLYHN DA7 ... 10 D1
Forest Rd ERITH DA8 ... 3 E3
Forge La EYN DA4 ... 33 E5
GVE DA12 ... 28 B1
GVE DA12 ... 29 G4
Forge Pl GVE * DA12 ... 19 F5
Fort Rd TIL RM18 ... 18 B1
Fortrye Cl GVW DA11 ... 26 C1
Fountain Wk GVW DA11 ... 17 G3
Fourth Av WTHK RM20 ... 6 A1
Foxendown La MEO DA13 ... 47 F4
Fox Manor Wy WTHK RM20 ... 6 B1
Foxton Rd WTHK RM20 ... 6 D1
Foxwood Gv GVW DA11 ... 17 G5
Foxwood Rd RDART DA2 ... 24 B2
Foxwood Wy HART DA3 ... 36 A3
Francis Rd DART DA1 ... 12 D2
Franklin Rd GVE DA12 ... 27 H4
Franks La EYN DA4 ... 42 D1
Fraser Cl BXLY DA5 ... 11 E5
Freeland Wy ERITH DA8 ... 3 E3
Freeman Rd GVE DA12 ... 28 A2
Freta Rd BXLYHS DA6 ... 10 B2
Frinsted Rd ERITH DA8 ... 2 B2
Frobisher Rd ERITH DA8 ... 3 E2
Frobisher Wy GRH DA9 ... 15 F1
GVE DA12 ... 28 A4
Fulwich Rd DART DA1 ... 13 F3
Furner Cl DART DA1 ... 2 D5

G

Gable Cl DART DA1 ... 12 A2
The Gables HART DA3 ... 36 A3
Gabriel Gdns GVE DA12 ... 28 A4
Gabrielspring Rd EYN DA4 ... 43 F5
Gabriel Spring Rd (East)
EYN DA4 ... 43 G5
Gainsborough Av DART DA1 ... 12 C2
TIL RM18 ... 9 E3
Gainsborough Dr GVW DA11 ... 26 B2
Galleon Bvd GRH DA9 ... 14 B1
Galley Hill Rd SWCM DA10 ... 16 B2
Galsworthy Rd TIL RM18 ... 9 G3
Garden Pl RDART DA2 ... 21 H2
Garden Rw GVW DA11 ... 26 D2
Garrick St GVW DA11 ... 18 B3
Garrolds Cl SWLY BR8 ... 30 B3
Garrow HART DA3 ... 35 H4
Gascoyne Dr DART DA1 ... 2 D5
Gasson Rd SWCM DA10 ... 16 A3
Gateway Pde GVE * DA12 ... 28 B3
Gatwick Rd GVE DA12 ... 27 F1
Gaylor Rd TIL RM18 ... 8 C3
Gazelle Gld GVE DA12 ... 28 B4
Geddes Pl BXLYHN DA7 ... 10 C1
Genesta Gld GVE DA12 ... 28 C4
George St GRAYS RM17 ... 7 G1
Gerald Rd GVE DA12 ... 19 E4
Gerdview Dr RDART DA2 ... 21 G3
Gibson Cl GVW DA11 ... 26 D2
Gilbert Cl SWCM DA10 ... 15 H3
Gilbert Rw GVW * DA11 ... 26 D1
Gildenhill Rd SWLY BR8 ... 31 G1
Gill Crs GVW DA11 ... 26 D2
Gillies Rd BGR/WK TN15 ... 50 C3
Gill's Rd EYN DA4 ... 33 G2
Gipsy La GRAYS RM17 ... 8 A1
The Glades GVE DA12 ... 27 H5
Gladstone Rd DART DA1 ... 13 F3
Glebelands DART DA1 ... 11 H1
Glebe Pl EYN DA4 ... 33 E5
Glebe Rd GVW DA11 ... 17 H5
Glebe Wy ERITH DA8 ... 2 C1
Glendale SWLY BR8 ... 40 D1
Glendale Rd GVW DA11 ... 26 C3
Glenhurst Av BXLY DA5 ... 10 B5
Glenrosa Gdns GVE DA12 ... 28 B4
Glen Vw GVE DA12 ... 18 C5
Gloucester Rd DART DA1 ... 12 B3
GVE DA12 ... 27 G3
Gloxinia Rd MEO DA13 ... 25 H5
Goldace GRAYS RM17 ... 7 F1
Goldsel Rd SWLY BR8 ... 30 C5
Goldsmith GRAYS RM17 ... 7 F1
Goldsmiths Whf GRAYS * RM17 ... 7 G2
Golf Links Av GVW DA11 ... 27 F4
Goodwood Crs GVE DA12 ... 27 G5
Gordon Pl GVE DA12 ... 18 C3
Gordon Prom East GVE DA12 ... 18 D3
Gordon Rd DART DA1 ... 12 D4
GVW DA11 ... 17 G4
Gore Rd RDART DA2 ... 23 F1
Gorringe Av EYN DA4 ... 33 F3
Gorse Wy HART DA3 ... 45 F1
Gorse Wood Rd HART DA3 ... 45 F1
Goss Hl SWLY BR8 ... 21 G5
Gothic Cl DART DA1 ... 21 H2
Gouge Av GVW DA11 ... 17 G5
Graham Rd BXLYHN DA7 ... 10 D1
Grain Terminal TIL * RM18 ... 8 A3
Granby Rd GVW DA11 ... 17 F3
Grange Crs RDART DA2 ... 13 H3
Grange La HART DA3 ... 45 H3
Grange Rd GRAYS RM17 ... 7 H1
GVW DA11 ... 18 A4

The Grange EYN DA4....33 F2
Grange Wy ERITH DA8....3 F2
  HART DA3....45 F2
Grangeways Cl GVW DA11....26 D3
Grangewood BXLY DA5....10 B5
Granville Rd GVW DA11....17 H4
Grasmere Rd BXLYHS DA7....2 A3
Gravel Hl BXLYHS DA6....10 D2
Gravel Hill Cl BXLY DA5....10 D3
Gravel Rd EYN DA4....32 D1
Gravesend Rd GVE DA12....29 G3
Graylands GRAYS * RM17....7 E1
Grazeley Cl BXLYHS DA6....11 E3
Great Queen St DART DA1....13 F3
Greenacre Cl SWLY BR8....30 C5
Greenbanks DART DA1....22 A1
Green Court Rd SWLY BR8....40 B1
Green Farm La GVE DA12....29 C2
Greenfield Rd RDART DA2....20 B4
Greenfinches HART DA3....35 H4
Greenhill Rd GVW DA11....26 D1
Green Lands GVE DA12....47 H1
Green La MEO DA13....47 F3
Greenside BXLY DA5....10 A5
  SWLY BR8....30 B3
Green Street Green Rd
  DART DA1....13 G5
  RDART DA2....23 E2
The Green RDART DA2....23 F1
Green Wk DART DA1....11 H1
Green Wy HART DA3....45 E1
Greenways HART DA3....36 B4
Greenwood Rd BXLY DA5....20 B3
Gresham Av HART DA3....35 F5
Gresham Cl BXLY DA5....10 A3
Greyhound Wy DART DA1....11 G2
Grieves Rd GVW DA11....26 D2
Griffin Wk GRH DA9....14 D2
Grosvenor Crs DART DA1....12 D2
Grosvenor Sq HART * DA3....35 E4
Grovebury Cl ERITH DA8....2 B1
Groveherst Rd DART DA1....4 B5
Grove Rd BXLYHN DA7....11 E1
  GRAYS RM17....8 A1
  GVW DA11....16 D2
The Grove GVE DA12....18 B4
  SWCM DA10....16 A2
  SWLY BR8....30 D4
Guild Rd ERITH DA8....2 D2
Gumley Rd WTHK RM20....6 D1
Gunfleet Cl GVE DA12....19 E4
Gun Hl TIL RM18....9 H1
Gunn Rd SWCM DA10....16 A3
Gwynn Rd GVW DA11....26 A1

H

Hadley Cl MEO DA13....47 F5
Hadlow Wy MEO DA13....36 C1
Haig Gdns GVE DA12....18 C4
Halcot Av BXLYHS DA6....10 D2
Haldane Gdns GVW DA11....17 E5
Halfpence La GVE DA12....38 D3
Hallford Wy DART DA1....12 C3
Hall Place Crs BXLY DA5....11 E2
Hall Rd DART DA1....13 F1
  GVW DA11....26 A2
Halstead Rd ERITH DA8....2 C3
Hamerton Rd GVW DA11....16 D2
Hampton Crs GVE DA12....28 A1
Handel Crs TIL RM18....9 E2
Hansol Rd BXLYHS DA6....10 A2
Harbex Cl BXLY DA5....10 D4
Harcourt Rd BXLYHS DA6....10 A1
Harden Rd GVW DA11....26 D1
Hardwick Crs DART DA1....13 H3
Hardy Av GVW DA11....26 C1
Hardy Gv DART DA1....13 G1
Harfst Wy SWLY BR8....30 A2
Harman Av GVW DA11....27 F4
Harmer Rd SWCM DA10....16 B3
Harmer St GVE DA12....18 C3
Harnetts Cl SWLY * BR8....40 B3
Harold Rd RDART DA2....22 B3
Harris Cl GVW DA11....26 C2
Harrowby Gdns GVW DA11....26 C1
Hart Dyke Rd SWLY BR8....30 B4
Hartford Rd BXLY DA5....10 C3
Hartlands Cl BXLY DA5....10 A5
Hartley Bottom Rd HART DA3....45 H4
Hartley Hl HART DA3....45 G4
Hartley Rd HART DA3....35 E3
Hart Shaw HART DA3....35 H3
Hartshill Rd GVW DA11....26 D1
Harvest Wy SWLY BR8....40 A3

Hasted Cl GRH DA9....15 G3
Hastings Cl WTHK RM20....7 E1
Hatton Cl GVW DA11....26 C2
Havelock Rd DART DA1....12 B4
  GVW DA11....17 H5
Haven Cl MEO DA13....36 D2
  SWLY BR8....30 D3
Havengore Av GVE DA12....19 E4
Haven Hl BGR/WK TN15....52 C4
Havisham Rd GVE DA12....19 G5
Hawkes Cl GRAYS RM17....7 H1
Hawkins Av GVE DA12....27 G3
Hawley Rd DART DA1....22 A1
Hawley Ter RDART * DA2....22 C3
Hawley V RDART * DA2....22 C4
Hawthorn Cl GVE DA12....27 F3
Hawthorn Rd BXLYHS * DA6....10 B1
  DART DA1....21 H1
Hawthorns HART DA3....35 F5
Hayes Cl WTHK RM20....6 C1
Hayes Rd RDART DA2....14 C4
Hayes Ter GVE * DA12....29 G4
Haynes Rd GVW DA11....26 D2
Hay Pl SWLY * BR8....40 A2
Hayward Cl DART DA1....11 F2
Hayward Dr DART * DA1....22 B2
Hazel Dr ERITH DA8....3 E3
Hazel End SWLY BR8....40 C1
Hazel Rd DART DA1....21 H1
  ERITH DA8....3 E3
Heath Cl SWLY BR8....30 C3
Heathclose Av DART DA1....12 B4
Heathclose Rd DART DA1....12 A5
Heathend Rd BXLY DA5....11 G5
Heatherbank Cl DART DA1....11 G3
Heather Dr DART DA1....12 A4
Heather End SWLY BR8....40 B1
Heathfield Cottages
  GRAYS * RM17....7 E1
Heathfield Rd BXLYHS DA6....10 B1
Heathfield Ter SWLY * BR8....30 B3
Heath Gdns DART * DA1....12 C5
Heathlands Ri DART DA1....12 B4
Heath La DART DA1....12 B5
Heathlee Rd DART DA1....21 H5
Heath Rd BXLY DA5....11 E5
  DART DA1....11 H3
Heath St DART DA1....12 D4
Heathview Av DART DA1....11 G3
Heathview Crs DART DA1....12 A4
Heath Wy ERITH DA8....2 A3
Heathwood Gdns SWLY BR8....30 A3
Heathwood Pde SWLY * BR8....30 A3
Heathwood Wk BXLY DA5....11 G5
Hedge Place Rd GRH DA9....14 C3
The Hedgerows GVW DA11....26 C1
Hedley Av WTHK RM20....6 C2
Helen Cl DART DA1....12 B4
Hemsted Rd ERITH DA8....2 C3
Henderson Dr DART DA1....13 G1
Henfield Cl BXLY DA5....10 C3
Hengist Rd ERITH DA8....2 A1
Hengrove Ct BXLY DA5....10 A5
Henhurst Rd MEO DA13....37 H3
Henley Deane GVW DA11....26 C3
Henry St GRAYS RM17....8 A1
Herbert Rd SWCM DA10....16 B3
  SWLY BR8....21 F5
Herongate Rd SWLY BR8....20 C5
Hesketh Av RDART DA2....13 H5
Hever Av BGR/WK TN15....50 C4
Hever Court Rd GVE DA12....27 G5
Hever Rd BGR/WK TN15....50 C4
Hever Wood Rd BGR/WK TN15....50 C5
Hewett Pl SWLY BR8....30 B5
Hibbs Cl SWLY BR8....30 B3
Hibernia Dr GVE DA12....28 B2
Highcross Rd MEO DA13....24 D5
Highfield Av ERITH * DA8....2 A1
Highfield Cottages SWLY * BR8....21 F5
Highfield Rd BXLYHS DA6....10 B2
  DART DA1....12 D4
Highfield Rd South DART DA1....12 D4
High Firs SWLY BR8....30 C5
Highland Gdns GVW DA11....26 C1
Highlands Hl SWLY BR8....31 E3
High Rd RDART DA2....21 F2
Highstead Crs ERITH DA8....2 C3
High St DART DA1....13 E3
  EYN DA4....42 B3
  EYN DA4....42 A5
  GRAYS RM17....7 G1
  GRH DA9....15 F1
  GVE DA12....18 B3
  GVW DA11....16 D3
  RDART DA2....24 B2
  SWCM DA10....16 B2
  SWLY BR8....30 C4

Highview Ter DART * DA1....12 D2
Hilda May Av SWLY BR8....30 C4
Hilden Dr ERITH DA8....3 F2
Hillary Av GVW DA11....26 C2
Hill Brow DART DA1....11 H3
Hillbrow Cl BXLY DA5....20 B3
Hill Cl MEO DA13....36 C1
Hill Crs BXLY DA5....11 E5
Hillcrest Av WTHK RM20....6 A1
Hillcrest Dr GRH DA9....15 E2
Hillcrest Rd DART DA1....11 G4
Hill House Rd RDART DA2....14 A4
Hillingdon Rd BXLYHN DA7....2 A5
  GVW DA11....27 F1
Hill Ri RDART DA2....22 A1
Hill Rd DART DA1....22 A1
Hill Shaw HART DA3....45 F2
Hillside EYN DA4....42 B3
  RDART DA2....23 E5
Hillside Av GVE DA12....27 H1
Hillside Ct SWLY BR8....31 E5
Hillside Dr GVE DA12....27 H1
Hillside Rd DART DA1....12 A3
Hillside Ter GVE * DA12....18 B5
The Hill GVW DA11....17 E3
Hilltop Gdns DART DA1....13 F2
Hilltop Rd WTHK RM20....6 A1
Hill View Rd HART DA3....35 H4
Hind Crs ERITH DA8....2 A2
Hind Ter WTHK * RM20....6 D1
Hive La GVW DA11....16 D2
Hobart Rd TIL RM18....9 E3
Hollands Cl GVE DA12....29 C4
The Hollies GVE DA12....27 H5
  HART DA3....36 A4
Hollybush Rd GVE DA12....27 C1
Holly Rd DART DA1....12 D5
Hollytree Av SWLY BR8....30 C3
Hollywood Wy ERITH DA8....3 F3
Holmesdale Hl EYN DA4....33 F2
Holmesdale Rd EYN DA4....35 E2
Holmleigh Av DART DA1....12 C1
Holmsdale Gv BXLYHN DA7....2 C4
Homefield Cl SWLY BR8....30 A3
Home Gdns DART DA1....13 E3
Home Hl SWLY BR8....30 D1
Homemead MEO * DA13....47 E2
Home Mead Cl GVE DA12....18 B4
Homer Cl BXLYHN DA7....2 C3
The Homestead DART DA1....12 C3
Hookfields GVW DA11....26 C2
Hook Green La RDART DA2....20 D2
Hook Green Rd MEO DA13....34 D1
Hope Rd SWCM DA10....16 B3
Hopewell Dr GVE DA12....28 B4
Horley Cl BXLYHS DA6....10 C2
Horsa Rd ERITH DA8....2 A2
Horsfield Cl RDART DA2....14 A4
Horsham Rd BXLYHS DA6....10 B3
Horsmans Pl DART * DA1....13 E4
Horton Rd EYN DA4....33 E4
Horton Wy EYN DA4....42 B3
Hoselands Vw HART DA3....35 E5
Hotham Cl SWLY BR8....31 F2
Hottsfield HART DA3....35 E4
Hove Cl GRAYS RM17....7 G1
Howard Rd DART DA1....13 G3
Howbury La ERITH DA8....3 E4
Howbury Rd DART DA1....3 E4
Howells Cl BGR/WK TN15....50 C4
Huggens College GVW * DA11....16 D2
Hulsewood Cl RDART DA2....21 F2
Humber Rd DART DA1....12 D2
Hume Av TIL RM18....9 F5
Hume Cl TIL RM18....9 F5
Hunters Cl BXLY DA5....20 C2
Huntingfield Rd MEO DA13....47 E3
Huntley Av GVW DA11....16 D3
Hunt Rd GVW DA11....26 C2
Hurlfield RDART DA2....21 G2
Hurst Pl DART * DA1....12 C3
Hurst Rd BXLY DA5....10 A5
  ERITH DA8....2 A2
Hurst Springs BXLY DA5....10 A5
Hurstwood Av BXLY DA5....10 A5
  BXLYHN DA7....2 C3
Hythe St DART DA1....13 E3

I

Idleigh Court Rd HART DA3....45 H5
Ifield Wy GVE DA12....27 H5
Imperial Dr GVE DA12....28 B4
Inglewood SWLY * BR8....30 C3
Inglewood Rd BXLYHN DA7....11 F1

Ingoldsby Rd GVE DA12....
Ingram Rd DART DA1....
Ingress Ter MEO * DA13....
Instone Rd DART DA1....
Invicta Rd RDART DA2....
Iris Av BXLY DA5....
Iron Mill La DART DA1....
Iron Mill Pl DART DA1....
Irving Wy SWLY BR8....
Istead Rd MEO DA13....
Ivy Bower Cl GRH DA9....
Ivy Cl DART DA1....
  GVE DA12....
Izane Rd BXLYHS DA6....

J

Jackson Cl GRH DA9....
Jagger Cl RDART DA2....
James Av BGR/WK * TN15....
James Rd DART DA1....
James Watt Wy ERITH DA8....
Jarrah Cottages PUR * RM19....
Jellicoe Av GVE DA12....
Jenningtree Rd ERITH DA8....
Jeskyns Rd MEO DA13....
Jessamine Pl RDART DA2....
Jessamine Ter SWLY * BR8....
Jetty Wk GRAYS RM17....
Johns Cl HART DA3....
Johnson Cl GVW DA11....
Johnsons Wy GRH DA9....
Johnsons Whf GRH * DA9....
John's Rd MEO DA13....
John St GRAYS RM17....
Josling Cl GRAYS RM17....
Joyce Green La DART DA1....
Joyden's Wood Rd BXLY DA5....
Joy Rd GVE DA12....
Jubilee Cl GRH DA9....
Jubilee Crs GVE DA12....
Jubilee Rd WTHK RM20....
Judeth Gdns GVE DA12....
Junction Rd DART DA1....
Jury St GVE DA12....

K

Keary Rd SWCM DA10....
Keats Gdns TIL RM18....
Keith Av GVE DA4....
Kelso Dr GVE DA12....
Kelvin Rd TIL RM18....
Kempton Cl ERITH DA8....
Kemsing Cl BXLY DA5....
Kemsley Cl GRH DA9....
  GVW DA11....
Kenley Cl BXLY DA5....
Kennet Rd DART DA1....
Kensington Ct GRAYS * RM17....
Kent Cl BGR/WK * TN15....
Kent Rd DART DA1....
  GRAYS RM17....
  GVW DA11....
  HART DA3....
Kenwood Av HART DA3....
Kenwyn Rd DART DA1....
Kettlewell Ct SWLY BR8....
Keyes Rd DART DA1....
Khartoum Pl GVE DA12....
Kilndown GVE DA12....
King Edward Av DART DA1....
King Edward Rd GRH DA9....
Kings Cl DART DA1....
Kingsdown Cl GVE DA12....
Kings Dr GVE DA12....
Kingsfield Ter DART * DA1....
Kingsingfield Cl BGR/WK TN15....
Kingsley Av DART DA1....
Kingsridge Gdns DART DA1....
Kingston Ct GVW DA11....
King St GVE DA12....
Kingswood Av SWLY BR8....
Kingswood Cl DART DA1....
Kipling Av TIL RM18....
Kipling Rd DART DA1....
Kirby Rd RDART DA2....
Kitchener Av GVE DA12....
Knatts Valley Rd RDART DA2....
Knights Cft HART DA3....
Knights Manor Wy DART DA1....
Knockhall Cha GRH DA9....
Knockhall Rd GRH DA9....
Knole Rd DART DA1....

...nole MEO DA13 ...... 36 C1
...Y BR8 ...... 30 B4
...num Av DART DA1 ...... 12 C5
...num Gv GVW DA11 ...... 17 F4
...Wy SWLY BR8 ...... 30 B5
...elds GVW DA11 ...... 26 D3
...ood Rd RDART DA2 ...... 23 G4
...la Wy DART DA1 ...... 12 C1
...ardes HART DA3 ...... 52 B1
...CI TIL RM18 ...... 9 C4
...na Av GVE DA12 ...... 27 H1
...ghters CI DART DA1 ...... 13 F3
...s CI MEO DA13 ...... 47 E3
...eer Av GVW DA11 ...... 26 B2
...GRH DA9 ...... 15 G3
...Av GVW DA11 ...... 26 D2
...fel CI HART DA3 ...... 35 E3
...nds Dr RDART DA2 ...... 23 G4
...orth CI RDART DA2 ...... 21 H2
...ry Crs DART DA1 ...... 13 G2
...owne Sq GVW DA11 ...... 17 H3
...wn PI GVW DA11 ...... 17 H5
...wn Rd TIL RM18 ...... 8 D4
...I GVE DA12 ...... 19 H5
...g CI ERITH * DA8 ...... 3 F2
...ngs HART DA3 ...... 35 H4
...d DART DA1 ...... 12 D5
...lds GVW DA11 ...... 26 C2
...ld HART DA3 ...... 35 F5
...ood CI ERITH DA8 ...... 3 E3
...ell La HART DA3 ...... 35 F5
...Rd ERITH DA8 ...... 2 D4
...n CI RDART DA2 ...... 23 G1
...n Rd BXLYHS DA6 ...... 10 C2
...n Dr GVE DA12 ...... 28 B4
...Dr SWLY BR8 ...... 31 E1
...Av GVE DA12 ...... 28 C2
...CI DART DA1 ...... 12 C5
...urels HART DA3 ...... 36 A4
...RT * DA2 ...... 21 G2
...ier HI SWLY BR8 ...... 30 A3
...e Rd DART DA1 ...... 13 F3
...d Gdns DART DA1 ...... 30 A3
...I SWLY BR8 ...... 30 A3
...d GVW DA11 ...... 17 E2
...Crs GRAYS RM17 ...... 8 B1
...PI GRAYS * RM17 ...... 8 B1
...nce Sq GVW * DA11 ...... 26 D2
...ce Dr GVE DA12 ...... 38 C5
...ace Gdns TIL RM18 ...... 9 F2
...ace Hill Gdns DART DA1 ...12 C3
...ce Hill Rd DART DA1 ...... 12 C5
...e Gdns DART DA1 ...... 12 D2
...Rd DART DA1 ...... 12 D1
...r Dr GVE DA12 ...... 28 B3
...ART DA1 ...... 11 F1
...roft Av SWLY BR8 ...... 30 B4
...od PI SWLY BR8 ...... 30 B5
...er Rd TIL RM18 ...... 8 D3
...RDART * DA2 ...... 22 C4
...d GVW DA11 ...... 27 F1
...n Gdns TIL RM18 ...... 9 E2
...ark Rd GVW DA11 ...... 18 B5
...Av GVW DA11 ...... 18 A3
...Rd GVW DA11 ...... 17 H3
...Rd East GVW DA11 ...... 18 A4
...I BXLYHS DA6 ...... 10 A1
...Av SWCM DA10 ...... 16 A4
...CI BXLY DA5 ...... 10 A4
...DA13 ...... 36 D2
...BR8 ...... 30 B4
...Pk ERITH DA8 ...... 2 B1
...Park Rd ERITH DA8 ...... 2 B1
...I GRAYS RM17 ...... 7 G1
...d BXLYHS DA6 ...... 10 A1
...d MEO DA13 ...... 36 D2
...DA13 ...... 16 A3
...Gdns ERITH DA8 ...... 3 F3
...natch La SWLY BR8 ...... 30 B2
...I SWLY BR8 ...... 40 C1
...h Av BXLYHN DA7 ...... 11 E1
...Cross Rd RDART DA2 ...... 20 D2
...ns SWLY BR8 ...... 30 B4
...MEO DA13 ...... 47 F3
...NLY BR8 ...... 30 B4
...GVW DA11 ...... 17 F4
...SWLY BR8 ...... 30 B4
...es EYN * DA4 ...... 42 B3
...e Av GRH DA9 ...... 15 G1
...ood Rd ERITH DA8 ...... 2 A2
...I ERITH DA8 ...... 2 D4

L

Lincoln Rd ERITH DA8 ...... 2 D4
Linden Av DART DA1 ...... 12 C5
Linden CI PUR RM19 ...... 5 E1
Lindisfarne CI GVE DA12 ...... 28 A1
Lingfield Rd RDART DA2 ...... 13 H4
Lingfield Rd GVE DA12 ...... 27 F1
Ling Rd ERITH DA8 ...... 2 A1
Links Vw DART DA1 ...... 12 C5
Lion Rd BXLYHS DA6 ...... 10 A1
Lisle CI GVE DA12 ...... 28 D1
Lister Rd TIL RM18 ...... 9 E4
Littlebrook Manor Wy
  DART DA1 ...... 13 G2
Littlecroft MEO DA13 ...... 36 C1
Little Queen St DART DA1 ...... 13 H4
Livingstone Gdns GVE DA12...27 H4
Livingstone Rd GVE DA12 ...... 27 H4
Lodge Av DART DA1 ...... 12 C3
Lodge Ct GVE DA12 ...... 29 G5
Lodge La GVE DA12 ...... 38 D5
Lombard St EYN DA4 ...... 33 E5
Londonderry Pde ERITH * DA8 ...2 B2
London Rd DART DA1 ...... 11 F2
  EYN DA4 ...... 41 H2
  GRAYS RM17 ...... 7 E1
  GRH DA9 ...... 14 C3
  GVW DA11 ...... 17 F3
  RDART DA2 ...... 14 A4
  SWCM DA10 ...... 16 A2
  SWLY BR8 ...... 30 A3
  TIL RM18 ...... 9 F4
  WTHK RM20 ...... 6 D1
London Rd Purfleet PUR RM19...4 D1
London Rd West Thurrock
  WTHK RM20 ...... 5 H1
Longfield Av HART DA3 ...... 36 A3
Longfield Rd MEO DA13 ...... 46 C1
Longmarsh Vw EYN DA4 ...... 32 D2
Longreach Rd ERITH DA8 ...... 3 F2
Longwalk MEO DA13 ...... 36 C2
Lonsdale Crs RDART DA2 ...... 23 E1
Lord St GVE DA12 ...... 18 B4
Lordswood CI RDART DA2 ...... 23 G3
Lorton CI GVE DA12 ...... 28 A1
Louvain Rd RDART DA2 ...... 14 C4
Lovelace CI BGR/WK TN15 ...... 50 C4
Love La BXLY DA5 ...... 10 C3
Lover's La GRH DA9 ...... 15 H1
Low CI GRH DA9 ...... 15 G2
Lower Cft SWLY BR8 ...... 30 D5
Lower Higham Rd GVE DA12 ...19 F5
Lower Range Rd GVE DA12 ...... 19 E4
Lower Rd GVE DA12 ...... 29 C1
  GVW DA11 ...... 16 C1
  SWLY BR8 ...... 31 F1
  TIL RM18 ...... 18 A1
Lower Station Rd DART DA1 ...11 C3
Lowfield St DART DA1 ...... 13 E4
Lullingstone Av SWLY BR8 ...... 30 D4
Lullingstone La EYN DA4 ...... 48 C1
Lunedale Rd RDART DA2 ...... 14 A5
Lydia Rd ERITH DA8 ...... 2 D1
Lynden Wy SWLY BR8 ...... 30 A4
Lyndhurst Wy MEO DA13 ...... 36 C2
Lynsted CI BXLYHS DA6 ...... 10 D2
Lynton Rd GVW DA11 ...... 18 A5
Lynton Rd South GVW DA11 ...18 A5

M

Mabel Rd SWLY BR8 ...... 21 E5
Mackenzie Wy GVE DA12 ...... 27 H5
Maclean Ter GVE * DA12 ...... 28 B1
Madden CI SWCM DA10 ...... 16 A3
Magnet Rd WTHK RM20 ...... 6 C1
Maida Vale Rd DART DA1 ...... 12 A3
Maiden Erlegh Av BXLY DA5 ...10 A5
Maiden La DART DA1 ...... 12 D5
Maidstone Rd GRAYS RM17 ...... 7 G1
Main Ga TIL * RM18 ...... 9 E4
Main Rd EYN DA4 ...... 22 D5
  EYN DA4 ...... 42 A2
  HART DA3 ...... 35 E3
  RDART DA2 ...... 34 C2
  SWLY BR8 ...... 30 D2
  SWLY BR8 ...... 40 A2
Main Rd Gorse HI EYN DA4 ...42 D4
Mallard CI DART DA1 ...... 12 A1
Mallow CI GVW DA11 ...... 26 C3
Mallow Ct GRAYS RM17 ...... 8 B1
Mallys PI EYN DA4 ...... 33 E2
Malta Rd TIL RM18 ...... 8 D1
Maithouse La GVE DA12 ...... 27 F1
Malvina Av GVE DA12 ...... 27 F1
Malyons Rd SWLY BR8 ...... 30 D1
Mannock Rd DART DA1 ...... 4 B5

Manor CI DART DA1 ...... 11 F1
  GVE DA12 ...... 28 D1
  RDART DA2 ...... 21 E2
Manor Ct MEO DA13 ...... 47 H1
Manor Dr HART DA3 ...... 45 G2
Manor Fld GVE DA12 ...... 29 G4
Manor Forstal HART DA3 ...... 52 B1
Manor La HART DA3 ...... 44 C3
  HART DA3 ...... 45 G2
Manor Rd BXLY DA5 ...... 10 D5
  DART DA1 ...... 11 G1
  ERITH DA8 ...... 2 D1
  GRAYS RM17 ...... 8 A1
  GVE * DA12 ...... 18 B3
  HART DA3 ...... 46 A1
  MEO DA13 ...... 47 G1
  SWCM DA10 ...... 15 H3
  TIL RM18 ...... 9 F2
  WTHK RM20 ...... 6 C1
Manor Vw HART * DA3 ...... 45 G2
Manor Wy BXLY DA5 ...... 10 C5
  BXLYHN DA7 ...... 2 B5
  GRAYS RM17 ...... 7 H2
  GVW DA11 ...... 17 E1
  SWCM DA10 ...... 16 A1
Manse Wy SWLY BR8 ...... 31 E5
Mansfield Rd SWLY BR8 ...... 20 C5
Maple CI SWLY BR8 ...... 30 C3
Maple Rd DART DA1 ...... 12 C5
  GRAYS RM17 ...... 8 A1
  GVE DA12 ...... 27 G3
Maplescombe La EYN DA4 ...... 49 G1
The Maples HART DA3 ...... 35 H4
Marcet Rd DART DA1 ...... 12 C2
Marconi Rd GVW DA11 ...... 26 B2
Marcus Rd DART DA1 ...... 12 A4
Marden Crs BXLY DA5 ...... 11 E2
Marie Manor Wy RDART * DA2 ...23 E2
Marina Dr DART DA1 ...... 13 G5
  GVW DA11 ...... 17 H4
Maritime CI GRH DA9 ...... 15 F2
Market PI DART DA1 ...... 13 E4
  TIL * RM18 ...... 9 E4
Market St DART DA1 ...... 13 E4
Mark La GVE DA12 ...... 19 E3
Marks Sq GVW DA11 ...... 26 D3
Mark Wy SWLY * BR8 ...... 41 E1
Marlborough Rd DART DA1 ...... 12 C3
Marling Wy GVE DA12 ...... 28 A4
The Marlowes DART DA1 ...... 11 F1
Marriott Rd DART DA1 ...... 13 G4
Marsh St DART DA1 ...... 4 C4
Martens Av BXLYHN DA7 ...... 11 E1
Martens CI BXLYHN DA7 ...... 11 E1
Martin Dene BXLYHS DA6 ...... 10 B2
Martin Ri BXLYHS DA6 ...... 10 B2
Martin Rd RDART DA2 ...... 21 G2
Maryfield CI BXLY DA5 ...... 20 C2
Masefield Rd ERITH DA8 ...... 2 D3
Masefield Rd DART DA1 ...... 13 H2
  GVW DA11 ...... 26 B2
Masthead CI GRH DA9 ...... 14 A1
Maude Rd SWLY BR8 ...... 21 E5
Maxim Rd DART DA1 ...... 11 G2
May Av RDART DA2 ...... 17 H5
Maybury Av RDART DA2 ...... 13 H5
Mayes CI SWLY BR8 ...... 31 E5
Mayfair Rd DART DA1 ...... 12 D3
Mayfield Rd SWCM DA10 ...... 16 A3
Mayfield Rd GVW DA11 ...... 17 H5
Maynard CI ERITH DA8 ...... 2 D2
Mayplace Av DART DA1 ...... 12 A1
Mayplace Rd BXLYHN DA7 ...... 2 A5
Mayplace Rd East BXLYHN DA7...2 A5
Mayplace Rd West BXLYHN DA7 ...10 D1
Maypole Crs ERITH DA8 ...... 3 H1
Maypole Rd GVE DA12 ...... 19 F5
May Rd RDART DA2 ...... 22 B3
McCudden Rd DART DA1 ...... 4 B5
McMillan CI GVE DA12 ...... 27 G3
Mead CI SWLY BR8 ...... 41 E1
Mead Crs DART DA1 ...... 12 D5
Meadfield Rd MEO DA13 ...... 47 E5
Meadow CI BXLYHS DA6 ...... 10 B2
Meadowcroft Farm
  RDART * DA2 ...... 34 B1
Meadow Rd GVW DA11 ...... 17 E1
  GVW DA11 ...... 27 E1
Meadowside DART DA1 ...... 13 H3
Meadow Vw SWLY * BR8 ...... 40 B2
Meadowview Rd BXLY DA5 ...... 10 A3
Meadow Wk RDART DA2 ...... 21 G3
Meadow Wy RDART DA2 ...... 14 A4
Mead Rd DART DA1 ...... 12 D5
  GVW DA11 ...... 17 E1
The Mead HART DA3 ...... 45 E5
Medbury Rd GVE DA12 ...... 19 F5
Medhurst Crs GVE DA12 ...... 28 B2

Medhurst Gdns GVE DA12 ...... 28 B2
Medick Ct GRAYS RM17 ...... 8 C1
Medlar Rd GRAYS RM17 ...... 8 B1
The Medlars MEO DA13 ...... 47 E2
Medway Rd DART DA1 ...... 3 F5
Melba Gdns TIL RM18 ...... 9 E2
Melbourne Rd TIL RM18 ...... 8 C3
Melliker La MEO DA13 ...... 46 D1
Mendip Rd BXLYHN DA7 ...... 2 C3
Meopham Ct MEO * DA13 ...... 47 H1
Mera Dr BXLYHN DA7 ...... 10 C1
Merewood Rd BXLYHN DA7 ...... 2 A4
Mermerus Gdns GVE DA12 ...... 28 B3
Merryfields CI HART DA3 ...... 35 F5
Merryweather CI DART DA1 ...13 F3
Merton Av HART DA3 ...... 35 E5
Methuen Rd BXLYHS DA6 ...... 10 B1
Meyer Rd ERITH DA8 ...... 2 A1
Michael Gdns GVE DA12 ...... 28 A5
Michaels La HART DA3 ...... 44 B5
Midfield Av BXLYHN DA7 ...... 2 A5
  SWLY BR8 ...... 21 E5
Midhurst HI BXLYHS DA6 ...... 10 C2
Mildred CI DART DA1 ...... 13 C3
Mile Stone Rd RDART DA2 ...... 13 H3
Millais PI TIL RM18 ...... 9 E2
Millbro SWLY BR8 ...... 31 E2
Miller Rd GVE DA12 ...... 28 C1
Millers Wk MEO DA13 ...... 47 E5
Millfield HART DA3 ...... 45 E5
Millfield Dr GVW DA11 ...... 26 C1
Millfield La HART DA3 ...... 45 E5
Mill Hill La GVE DA12 ...... 29 F4
Mill La EYN DA4 ...... 42 A4
Mill PI DART DA1 ...... 12 A1
Mill Pond Rd DART DA1 ...... 13 E3
Mill Rd ERITH DA8 ...... 2 D1
  GVW DA11 ...... 17 C4
  PUR RM19 ...... 4 D1
  RDART DA2 ...... 22 B3
Mill Rw BXLY * DA5 ...... 10 D5
Mill Stone CI EYN DA4 ...... 33 E3
Millstone Ms EYN DA4 ...... 33 E2
Milroy Av GVE DA12 ...... 26 C1
Milton Av GVE DA12 ...... 18 D5
Milton Gdns TIL RM18 ...... 9 F3
Milton Hall Rd GVE DA12 ...... 18 D5
Milton PI GVE DA12 ...... 18 C3
Milton Rd GVE DA12 ...... 18 B3
  SWCM DA10 ...... 16 A3
Milton St SWCM DA10 ...... 15 H3
Miskin Rd DART DA1 ...... 12 C4
Miskin Wy GVE DA12 ...... 27 H5
Mitchell Av GVW DA11 ...... 26 B1
Mitchell CI DART DA1 ...... 22 A1
Mitchem CI BGR/WK TN15 ...... 50 C5
Moat La ERITH DA8 ...... 3 E3
Mollison Ri GVE DA12 ...... 28 A4
Monarch CI TIL RM18 ...... 9 F4
Monks Orch DART DA1 ...... 21 G1
Monks Wk MEO DA13 ...... 25 C5
Montague CI SWLY BR8 ...... 30 D5
Montague PI SWLY * BR8 ...... 30 D5
Monterey CI BXLY DA5 ...... 20 A1
Montgomery Rd EYN DA4 ...... 33 F2
Montreal Rd TIL RM18 ...... 9 E5
Moore Av TIL RM18 ...... 9 F4
Moore Rd SWCM DA10 ...... 16 A3
Moorhen CI ERITH DA8 ...... 3 F2
Morello CI SWLY BR8 ...... 30 B5
Moreton Ct DART DA1 ...... 21 G1
Morgan Dr RDART DA2 ...... 14 C4
Morland Av DART DA1 ...... 12 B2
Mornington Ct BXLY DA5 ...... 11 F5
Morris Gdns DART DA1 ...... 13 G2
Mortimer Rd ERITH DA8 ...... 2 B1
Moss Wy RDART DA2 ...... 23 F3
Moultain HI SWLY BR8 ...... 31 E5
Mount Cottages BXLYHS * DA6 ...10 A1
Mount Pleasant Rd DART DA1...13 F3
Mount Rd BXLYHS DA6 ...... 10 A2
  DART DA1 ...... 11 H3
Mounts Rd GRH DA9 ...... 15 F3
The Mount BXLYHS * DA6 ...... 10 A1
Mulberry CI MEO DA13 ...... 47 F2
Mulberry Rd GVW DA11 ...... 26 C3
Mullein Ct GRAYS RM17 ...... 8 B1
Multon Rd BGR/WK TN15 ...... 50 C4
Munford Dr SWCM DA10 ...... 16 B4
Mungo Park Rd GVE DA12 ...... 27 H4
Mussenden La EYN DA4 ...... 43 F2
Myrtle CI ERITH DA8 ...... 2 C2
Myrtle PI RDART DA2 ...... 14 B5
Myrtle Rd DART DA1 ...... 21 H1

N

Nairn Ct *TIL* * RM18 ....8 D4
Nansen Rd *GVE* DA12 ....27 H3
Napier Rd *GVW* DA11..................17 H5
Nash Bank *MEO* DA13..................36 D3
Nash Cft *MEO* DA13....................26 C3
Nash St *MEO* DA13.......................37 E3
Neal Rd *BGR/WK* TN15..............50 C4
Nelson Rd *DART* DA1..................12 C3
   GVW DA11 ....26 D1
Ness Rd *ERITH* DA8 ....3 H1
Neville Pl *MEO* * DA13...............47 E1
New Barn Rd *HART* DA3 ....35 H4
   MEO DA13 ....25 H3
   MEO DA13 ....26 A4
   SWLY BR8 ....30 C2
Newbery Rd *ERITH* DA8 ....2 D3
New House La *GVW* DA11.........26 D2
Newick Cl *BXLY* DA5....................10 D3
Newman's Rd *GVW* DA11...........26 D1
Newports *SWLY* BR8...................40 B3
New Rd *EYN* DA4.........................33 E3
   GRAYS RM17 ....7 G1
   GVW DA11 ....18 A3
   MEO DA13 ....46 D1
   SWLY BR8 ....30 D4
   SWLY BR8 ....30 D1
New St *BGR/WK* TN15................53 F4
New Street Rd *BGR/WK* TN15....53 E1
New Swan Yd *GVE* * DA12 ....18 B3
Newton Abbot Rd *GVW* DA11 ...26 D1
Newton Rd *TIL* RM18.....................9 E4
Newton's Ct *GRH* DA9................14 B1
Nickleby Rd *GVE* DA12 ....19 C5
Nightingale Cl *GVW* DA11 ....26 C3
Nightingale Wy *SWLY* BR8 ....30 C4
Nine Elms Gv *GVW* DA11............18 A4
Norfield Rd *RDART* DA2 ....20 A3
Norfolk Cl *DART* DA1..................13 G3
Norfolk Rd *GVE* DA12.................18 D3
Normandy Wy *ERITH* DA8.............2 C3
Norman Rd *DART* DA1.................13 E5
Normans Cl *GVW* DA11 ....18 A4
Norris Wy *DART* DA1.....................2 D5
Northall Rd *BXLYHN* DA7 ....2 A4
Northcote Rd *GVW* DA11 ....17 H5
Northdown Rd *HART* DA3 ....35 E3
Northend Rd *ERITH* DA8...............2 D3
Northfield *HART* DA3..................35 F4
North Kent Av *GVW* DA11 ....17 E3
Northridge Rd *GVE* DA12...........27 G2
North Riding *HART* DA3..............36 B4
North Rd *DART* DA1....................11 H3
North St *BXLYHN* DA7................10 C1
   DART DA1 ....12 D4
   GVE DA12 ....18 B4
Northumberland Cl *ERITH* DA8 ...2 A2
Northumberland Pk *ERITH* DA8 ...2 A2
Northumberland Av *MEO* DA13 ...36 D1
Northumberland Wy
   BXLYHN DA7 ....2 A3
Northview *SWLY* BR8 ....30 C3
North View Av *TIL* RM18...............9 E3
Norwich Pl *BXLYHS* DA6.............10 C1
Norwood La *MEO* DA13..............47 F1
Nuffield Rd *SWLY* BR8................21 E5
Nursery Cl *RDART* DA2 ....14 A4
   SWLY BR8 ....30 A3
Nursery Rd *MEO* DA13...............47 E1
The Nursery *ERITH* DA8................2 D2
Nurstead Av *HART* DA3 ....36 B4
Nurstead Church La *MEO* DA13 ..37 E5
Nurstead La *HART* DA3 ....36 B5
Nutbrook *HART* DA3...................35 H4
Nutley Cl *SWLY* BR8...................30 D2
Nutmead Cl *BXLY* DA5...............11 E5

O

Oak Cl *DART* DA1........................11 G1
Oakdene Av *ERITH* DA8................2 A1
Oakfield La *RDART* DA2..............21 E1
Oakfield Park Rd *DART* DA1.......21 H1
Oakfield Pl *DART* DA1................21 H1
Oakhouse Rd *BXLYHS* DA6........10 C2
Oaklands *BGR/WK* TN15............50 C4
   BXLYHS DA6.............................10 B2
Oaklands Rd *BXLYHS* DA6..........10 B1
   GVW DA11 ....26 D3
   RDART DA2 ....13 H5
Oakleigh Cl *SWLY* BR8...............30 C4
Oakley Cl *WTHK* RM20.................6 C1
Oakmead *MEO* DA13...................47 E5

Oak Rd *ERITH* DA8 ....2 A2
   ERITH DA8 ....3 E3
   GRAYS RM17 ....8 A1
   GRH DA9....................................14 C3
   GVE DA12 ....27 F2
The Oaks *SWLY* BR8 ....30 C3
Oak Tree Av *GRH* DA9................14 D4
Oakway Cl *BXLY* DA5..................10 A3
Oakwood Cl *DART* DA1...............13 H5
Oakwood Dr *BXLYHN* DA7.........11 E1
Oast Wy *HART* DA3.....................35 E4
Oast Wy *HART* DA3.....................45 E2
Old Barn Wy *BXLYHN* DA7.........11 F1
Old Bexley La *BXLY* DA5.............20 B1
Old Chapel Rd *SWLY* BR8...........40 A3
Old Dartford Rd *EYN* DA4...........42 B2
Old Downs *HART* DA3.................45 E1
Old Farm Gdns *SWLY* BR8.........30 D4
Old Manor Wy *BXLYHN* DA7........2 B4
Old Mill Cl *EYN* DA4....................42 A4
Old Perry St *GVW* DA11.............26 C1
Old Rd *DART* DA1........................11 F1
Old Rd East *GVE* DA12...............18 D5
Old Rd West *GVW* DA11.............17 H5
Old School Ct *SWLY* * BR8.........30 C3
The Old Yews *HART* DA3............35 H4
Oliver Cl *WTHK* RM20...................5 H2
Oliver Crs *EYN* DA4....................42 B3
Olive Rd *DART* DA1.....................12 D5
Oliver Rd *SWLY* BR8...................30 B4
   WTHK RM20 ....5 H3
Optima Pk *DART* * DA1................3 E5
Orbital One *DART* * DA1.............22 D1
Orchard Av *DART* DA1................12 B4
   GVW DA11 ....27 F4
Orchard Cl *HART* DA3.................35 H3
Orchard Dr *MEO* DA13................46 D1
Orchard Hl *DART* DA1.................11 G2
Orchard Lea *MEO* * DA13...........25 F3
Orchard Rd *GVW* DA11...............26 A1
   SWCM DA10 ....16 A2
Orchard St *DART* DA1.................13 E3
Orchard Ter *GRH* * DA9..............14 C2
The Orchard *SWLY* BR8..............30 B3
Orchard Wy *RDART* DA2.............21 H2
Ordnance Rd *GVE* DA12.............18 C3
Orlick Rd *GVE* DA12....................28 D1
Osbourne Rd *RDART* DA2...........13 H3
Osney Wy *GVE* DA12..................28 B1
Osterberg Rd *DART* DA1.............13 F1
Otford Cl *BXLY* DA5....................10 D3
Ottawa Rd *TIL* RM18.....................9 E4
The Oval *HART* DA3....................36 A4
Overcliffe *GVW* DA11..................18 A3
Overmead *SWLY* BR8..................40 C1
Over Minnis *HART* DA3...............52 B1
Overy Liberty *DART* DA1.............13 C4
Overy St *DART* DA1....................13 F3
Oxford Cl *GVE* DA12...................28 B1
Oxford Ms *BXLY* DA5..................10 C5

P

Pacific Cl *SWCM* DA10................16 A2
Packham Rd *GVW* DA11.............26 D2
Paddock Cl *EYN* DA4...................33 E2
Paddock Rd *BXLYHS* DA6...........10 A1
Pageant Cl *TIL* RM18....................9 G3
Page Cl *RDART* DA2....................24 C2
Page Crs *ERITH* DA8.....................2 D2
Painters Ash La *GVW* DA11........26 B2
Palmer Av *GVE* DA12..................27 H3
Panter's *SWLY* BR8.....................30 D1
The Parade *DART* * DA1..............11 H2
   GVE * DA12...............................27 H1
   HART * DA3...............................45 E1
   MEO * DA13 ....47 E3
   SWCM * DA10............................16 B2
Park Av *GVW* DA11.....................17 G5
   WTHK RM20 ....6 A1
Park Corner Rd *MEO* DA13.........25 F3
Park Crs *ERITH* DA8......................2 A1
Park Dr *HART* DA3......................35 E4
Parker Av *TIL* RM18......................9 G3
Park Gv *BXLYHN* DA7.................11 E1
Park Hl *MEO* DA13.......................36 C5
Parkhill Rd *BXLY* DA5.................10 B4
Parkhurst Gdns *BXLY* DA5.........10 C4
Parkhurst Rd *BXLY* DA5.............10 C4
Park La *SWLY* BR8......................31 G3
Park Pl *GVE* DA12.......................18 C3
Park Rd *DART* DA1......................13 G4
   GVW DA11 ....27 F1
   SWCM DA10 ....16 A3
   SWLY BR8 ....30 D5
Parkside Av *BXLYHN* DA7............2 B4

Parkside Cross *BXLYHN* DA7........2 C4
Parkside Pde *DART* * DA1.............2 D4
Park Ter *GRH* DA9.......................15 G2
Park Wallis *GVW* DA11...............16 D2
Park Wy *BXLY* DA5.....................20 D2
Parkwood Rd *BXLY* DA5.............10 B4
Parrock Av *GVE* DA12.................18 C5
Parrock Rd *GVE* DA12................18 C4
Parrock St *GVE* DA12.................18 B3
Parsonage La *EYN* DA4...............22 D5
Parsonage Rd *WTHK* RM20..........6 C1
Parsons La *RDART* DA2..............21 F2
Patterdale Rd *RDART* DA2..........14 A5
Peach Cft *GVW* DA11..................26 C2
Peacock St *GVE* DA12.................18 C4
Peareswood Rd *ERITH* DA8..........2 D3
Pearson Wy *DART* DA1...............22 B1
Pear Tree Cl *BXLYHN* DA7............2 B3
Pease Hl *BGR/WK* TN15..............52 B4
Pegasus Ct *GVE* DA12.................27 G2
Pelham Cottages *BXLY* * DA5....10 D5
Pelham Rd *GVW* DA11................17 H4
Pelham Rd South *GVW* DA11......17 H5
Pemberton Gdns *SWLY* BR8.......30 C4
Pembroke Pl *EYN* DA4................32 D2
Pencroft Dr *DART* DA1................12 C4
Penenden *HART* DA3...................45 F5
Penney Cl *DART* DA1..................13 E4
Pennine Wy *BXLYHN* DA7............2 B3
   GVW DA11 ....26 C2
Penshurst Cl *BGR/WK* TN15.......50 C4
   HART DA3 ....36 B3
Pentstemon Dr *SWCM* DA10.......16 A2
Pepper Hl *GVW* DA11..................26 A2
Pepys Cl *GVW* DA11....................26 B2
   TIL RM18....................................9 G3
Percy St *GRAYS* RM17..................8 A1
Perkins Cl *GRH* DA9....................14 D1
Perran Cl *HART* DA3...................35 F5
Perry Gv *DART* DA1.....................13 C1
Perry St *DART* DA1........................2 C5
   GVW DA11 ....17 G5
Pescot Av *HART* DA3..................35 C4
Petworth Rd *BXLYHS* DA6..........10 C2
Phelps Cl *BGR/WK* TN15............50 C4
Phillip Av *SWLY* BR8...................30 B5
Phillips Cl *DART* DA1..................12 B3
Phoenix Pl *DART* DA1..................12 D4
Pickwick Gdns *GVW* DA11..........26 B2
Pier Rd *ERITH* DA8.......................2 D1
   GRH DA9....................................15 F1
   GVW DA11 ....17 H3
Pier Whf *GRAYS* * RM17...............7 G2
Pilgrims Ct *DART* DA1................13 H3
Pilgrims' Rd *SWCM* DA10...........16 A1
Pilgrims Vw *GRH* DA9.................15 H5
Pilgrims Wy *DART* DA1...............13 H5
Pilots Pl *GVE* DA12.....................18 C3
Pincott Rd *BXLYHS* DA6.............10 C3
Pincroft Wd *HART* DA3...............36 A5
Pine Av *GVE* DA12......................18 D5
Pine Cl *SWLY* BR8......................30 D5
Pine Ri *MEO* DA13......................47 E2
Pinks Hl *SWLY* BR8.....................40 C1
Pinnacle Hl *BXLYHN* DA7............10 D1
Pinnock's Av *GVW* DA11............18 B5
Pioneer Wy *SWLY* BR8................30 C4
The Pippins *MEO* DA13...............47 E2
Pirrip Cl *GVE* DA12.....................19 F5
Pitfield *HART* DA3.......................35 F5
Pitfield Dr *MEO* DA13..................53 H1
Plane Av *GVW* DA11....................17 F4
Plantation Cl *GRH* DA9...............14 D2
Plantation Rd *ERITH* DA8.............3 E3
   SWLY BR8 ....31 E1
Polegate Cottages *WTHK* * RM20 ..7 E1
Pollyhaugh *EYN* DA4...................49 E1
Pondfield La *GVE* DA12..............39 C1
Poplar Av *GVE* DA12...................27 G3
Poplars Cl *HART* DA3..................36 A4
Poplar Wk *MEO* DA13.................47 F2
Porchester Cl *HART* DA3............35 F5
Porchfield Cl *GVE* DA12.............27 F5
Port Av *GRH* DA9........................15 F3
Porter Cl *WTHK* RM20...................6 C1
Portland Av *GVE* DA12...............27 F1
Portland Pl *HART* * DA3.............35 E4
Portland Rd *GVW* DA11...............17 F3
   GVW DA11 ....18 B5
Portman Cl *BXLY* DA5................11 C5
Portsea Rd *TIL* RM18....................9 G3
Pottery Rd *BXLY* DA5..................20 A1
Powder Mill La *DART* DA1...........22 A1
Powell Av *RDART* DA2................23 G1
Poynder Rd *TIL* RM18...................9 F3

Preston Rd *GVW* DA11...............
Primrose Ter *GVE* * DA12...........
Prince Charles Av *EYN* DA4........
Princes Av *RDART* DA2...............
Princes Rd *DART* DA1.................
   GVE DA12 ....
   RDART DA2 ....
   SWLY BR8 ....
Princesses Pde *DART* * DA1.......
Princes St *GVW* DA11.................
Princes Vw *DART* DA1.................
Priory Cl *DART* DA1....................
Priory Flds *EYN* DA4...................
Priory Gdns *DART* DA1...............
Priory Hl *DART* DA1....................
Priory La *EYN* DA4......................
Priory Pl *DART* DA1.....................
Prospect Gv *GVE* DA12...............
Prospect Pl *DART* DA1................
   GRAYS * RM17 ....
   GVE DA12 ....
Providence St *GRH* DA9..............
Puddledock La *RDART* DA2.........
Punch Cft *HART* DA3...................
Purfleet Deep Whf *PUR* * RM19 ..

Q

Quakers Cl *HART* DA3..................
Quantock Rd *BXLYHN* DA7..........
Quarry Wy *WTHK* RM20...............
Quay La *GRH* DA9.......................
Quebec Rd *TIL* RM18...................
Queen Elizabeth II Br *GRH* DA9 ..
Queen's Farm Rd *GVE* DA12.......
Queens Gdns *RDART* DA2............
Queens Rd *ERITH* DA8................
   GVE DA12 ....
Queen St *ERITH* * DA8................
   GVE DA12 ....
Questor *DART* * DA1....................

R

Rabbits Rd *EYN* DA4....................
Rablus Pl *EYN* * DA4...................
Racefield Cl *GVE* DA12................
Raeburn Av *DART* DA1................
Railway St *GVW* DA11.................
Raleigh Cl *ERITH* DA8.................
Ramsden Rd *ERITH* DA8..............
Randall Cl *ERITH* DA8.................
Randolph Cl *BXLYHN* DA7...........
Ranelagh Gdns *GVW* DA11..........
Range Rd *GVE* DA12...................
Ranworth Cl *ERITH* DA8..............
Raphael Av *TIL* RM18..................
Raphael Rd *GVE* DA12.................
Rashleigh Wy *EYN* DA4...............
Rathmore Rd *GVW* DA11.............
Ravensbourne Rd *DART* DA1.......
Ravenswood *BXLY* DA5...............
Rayford Cl *DART* DA1...................
Ray Lamb Wy *ERITH* DA8............
Rays Hl *EYN* DA4........................
Read Wy *GVE* DA12.....................
Rectory Cl *DART* DA1..................
Rectory Meadow *MEO* DA13.......
Rectory Rd *BGR/WK* TN15..........
   SWCM DA10 ....
   TIL RM18....................................
Redding Cl *RDART* DA2...............
Reddy Rd *ERITH* DA8..................
Redhill Rd *BGR/WK* TN15............
Redhill Wd *HART* DA3.................
Red Lodge Crs *BXLY* DA5...........
Red Lodge Rd *BXLY* DA5.............
Red St *MEO* DA13.......................
Reeves Crs *SWLY* BR8................
Regency Cl *BGR/WK* TN15..........
The Retreat *GRAYS* RM17............
Ribblesdale Rd *RDART* DA2.........
Richardson Cl *GRH* DA9..............
Richmer Rd *ERITH* DA8...............
Richmond Gv *GRAYS* RM17.........
Ridge Av *DART* DA1....................
Ridgecroft Cl *BXLY* DA5..............
The Ridge *BXLY* DA5...................
Ridge Wy *DART* DA1...................
Ridgeway *RDART* DA2.................
Ridgeway Av *GVE* DA12..............
The Ridgeway *GVE* DA12.............

wood *MEO* DA13 ....36 A2
s Market *DART* * DA1 ....13 E4
se *DART* DA1 ....11 H1
DA12..28 A3
ale Rd *BXLY* DA5................10 B4
dale *GVW* DA11 ....26 C1
ide *EYN* DA4........................41 H5
de Wy *DART* DA1 ....13 E2
iew Rd *GRH* * DA9 ....15 E2
Hood La *BXLYHS* DA6........10 A2
la Av *GVW* DA11 ....17 F4
s Cft *GVW* DA11...................26 C2
ster Dr *BXLY* DA5 ....13 G4
ster Rd *DART* DA1...............13 G4
DA12..28 B1
ster Wy *DART* DA1 ....11 H1
Cl *ERITH* DA8 ....3 F3
mpton Cl *GVW* DA12 ....19 E4
s Ct *SWLY* BR8....................31 E5
s Wood La *BGR/WK* TN15...51 E2
d *SWLY* BR8..........................30 D1
t Rd *GVW* DA11 ....24 B1
RT DA2...24 B1
n Villa Rd *EYN* DA4.............23 E5
n Wy *DART* DA1 ....11 G2
ry Ct *WTHK* * RM20..............6 A1
okery *WTHK* RM20.................6 A1
y *GVE* DA12 ....19 E5
nk Gdns *GVW* DA11............17 G5
erry Gdns *DART* DA1...........12 C4
ery Ct *GVW* DA11.................17 H5
ry Rd *GRAYS* RM17 ....7 E1
ale Cl *RDART* DA2 ....13 H4
ene Cl *DART* DA1 ....12 C1
arth *MEO* DA13 ....36 C2
a *GVW* DA11 ....16 D3
ood *RDART* DA2 ....20 C3
ville Wy *GVW* DA11 ....17 G3
Rd *TIL* RM18..........................8 D4
nd Cl *BXLYHS* DA6...............10 A2
d *DART* DA1 ....12 A3
La *GVE* DA12 ....18 C3
Ash Wy *HART* DA3................45 E2
St *MEO* DA13........................37 G4
Cl *MEO* DA13 ....47 F2
Crs *DART* DA1 ....12 C3
Rd *SWLY* BR8........................30 B4
s Cl *HART* DA3......................34 D3
Rd *RDART* DA2 ....21 E4
t Cl *RDART* DA2 ....21 G3
arsh Cl *GVW* DA11...............26 D2
Rd *SWLY* BR8........................20 D5
ak Rd *BXLYHS* DA6 ....10 A2
ier Rd *DART* DA1 ....18 B3
d *DART* DA1.........................17 H5
errace Pier *GVE* * DA12 .....18 C3
n Rd *DART* DA1 ....11 H3
GVW DA11 ....17 G4
s Rd *BGR/WK* TN15..............50 B5
GV *DART* DA1 ....13 G2
Cl *BXLYHN* DA7 ....10 C1
DA1...3 E5
Pl *EYN* DA4............................32 C2
Rd *GVE* DA12 ....3 C3
18..8 C3
Ter *EYN* * DA4 ....33 E5
sets *MEO* DA13.....................47 E2
Wy *SWLY* BR8.......................30 B3
Cl *DART* DA1 ....12 D4
Cl *SWLY* BR8.........................30 C4
Ct *SWLY* BR8.........................30 C4
Y *DA5
t *GVE* DA12 ....28 A4
DA3...36 B5

S

e Rd *DART* DA1....................21 H1
ton St *GVE* DA12 ....18 B4
s Hall *EYN* * DA4...................48 D1
s Pk *EYN* DA4........................44 D1
's Wy *GVE* DA12 ....28 A2
's Cl *GVE* DA12 ....27 H2
's Gdns *GVE* DA12 ....27 H2
's Rd *DART* DA1....................13 F3
w's Rd *GVE* * DA12 ....17 E4
18..8 C4
ict's Av *GVE* DA12................28 A2
gh Rd *GVW* DA11 ....26 B2
s Rd *TIL* RM18.......................9 E3
nt's Av *WTHK* RM20 ....6 A1
 nts Cl *GVW* * DA11 ....6 C2
ent's Rd *WTHK* RM20 ....6 C2
ba's Cl *GVE* DA12 ....28 A2

St David's Crs *GVE* DA12 ....27 H3
St David's Rd *SWLY* BR8.........20 D5
St Dunstan's Dr *GVE* DA12.....28 A2
St Edmunds Rd *DART* DA1 .....13 F1
St Francis La *DART* DA1 ....28 A3
St George's Crs *GVE* DA12......27 H3
St Georges Rd *SWLY* BR8........30 D5
St Gregory's Crs *GVE* DA12.....28 A1
St Hilda's Wy *DART* DA1 ....27 H3
St James' La *RDART* DA2 ....14 C4
St James Oaks *GVW* * DA11 ....18 A4
St James Pl *GVW* DA11...........12 D3
St James's Av *GVW* DA11 ....18 A4
St James's Rd *GVW* DA11 ....18 A3
St James's St *GVW* DA11 ....18 A3
St John's La *HART* DA3...........45 F2
St John's Rd *GVE* DA12...........18 D4
RDART DA2.....................................14 A4
St Leonards Cl *GRAYS* RM17......7 F1
St Lukes Cl *RDART* DA2 ....23 G4
SWLY BR8...30 B3
St Margarets Cl *RDART* DA2....23 F1
St Margaret's Crs *GVE* DA12....28 A2
St Margaret's Rd *EYN* DA4......33 G1
St Mark's Av *GVW* DA11 ....17 G4
St Martins Dr *EYN* DA4...........48 D1
St Martin's Rd *DART* DA1 ....13 F3
St Mary's Cl *GRAYS* * RM17 ......8 B1
GVE DA12.......................................27 G1
St Mary's Rd *BXLY* DA5...........11 E5
GRH DA9...14 C2
SWLY BR8...30 B5
St Marys Wy *HART* DA3...........35 E4
St Patrick's Gdns *GVE* DA12....27 H3
St Paul's Cl *SWCM* DA10.........16 A4
St Paul's Rd *ERITH* DA8 ....2 D3
St Peter's Cl *SWCM* DA10 ....16 B4
St Thomas Ct *BXLY* DA5..........10 C4
St Thomas Rd *GVW* * DA11 .....17 C5
St Thomas's Av *GVW* DA11 .....27 F1
St Thomas's Pl *GRAYS* RM17 ....8 A1
St Thomas Well *GVE* * DA12 ...38 C2
St Vincents Rd *DART* DA1 ....13 G3
Salcote Rd *GVE* DA12..............28 A4
Salem Pl *GVW* DA11................17 F4
Salisbury Av *SWLY* BR8 ....31 E5
Salisbury Rd *BXLY* DA5 ....10 C5
GRAYS RM17....................................8 A1
GVW DA11 ....17 H5
RDART DA2.....................................14 A5
Salix Rd *GRAYS* RM17................8 B1
Sallows Shaw *MEO* DA13.........47 G1
Salmon Rd *DART* DA1 ....4 B5
Samphire Ct *GRAYS* RM17........8 C1
Sanctuary Cl *DART* DA1...........12 C3
Sandbanks Hl *RDART* DA2.......24 C5
Sandford Rd *BXLYHS* DA6 ....10 A1
Sandhurst Rd *TIL* RM18............9 G4
Sandown Rd *GVE* DA12............27 G5
Sandpiper Dr *ERITH* DA8...........3 F2
The Sandpipers *GVE* DA12.......27 H1
Sandpit Rd *DART* DA1 ....12 C1
Sandy Bank Rd *GVE* DA12.......18 B5
Sandy La *CDW/CHF* RM16..........9 F1
MEO DA13.......................................25 E3
RDART DA2.....................................24 D2
WTHK RM20......................................6 A1
Sapho Pk *GVE* DA12................28 B3
Sara Crs *GRH* DA9...................15 E1
Sara Pk *GVE* DA12...................28 A3
Sarsens Cl *GVE* DA12...............38 B4
Saunders Cl *DART* DA1............26 C1
Saunders Wy *DART* DA1 ....22 B1
Savoy Rd *DART* DA1.................12 C2
Saxon Cl *GVW* DA11................26 A2
Saxon Pl *EYN* DA4....................43 E1
Saxon Rd *RDART* DA2..............22 A3
Saxon Shore Wy *GVE* DA12.....18 C3
Sayer Cl *GRH* DA9....................15 E2
School Cl *DART* DA1.................11 H1
MEO DA13.......................................47 E3
Schoolfield Rd *WTHK* RM20......6 A1
School La *EYN* DA4...................43 H2
RDART DA2.....................................24 C2
SWLY BR8...31 F1
School Rd *GVE* DA12................27 G2
Schooner Ct *DART* DA1 ....14 A1
Scotland La *GVE* DA12.............38 B4
Scott Crs *ERITH* DA8..................2 D3
Scott Rd *GVE* DA12..................27 H1
Scratchers La *EYN* DA4............50 B1
Scratton Flds *GVE* DA12..........47 H1
Scudders Hl *HART* DA3............44 C2
Seaton Rd *DART* DA1...............12 A4
Second Av *WTHK* RM20 ....6 A1
Sedley *MEO* DA13....................25 G4
Selah Dr *SWLY* BR8..................30 A2

Selborne Av *BXLY* DA5 ....10 A5
Selbourne Cl *HART* DA3..........36 B5
Selkirk Dr *ERITH* DA8................2 C5
Selwyn Rd *TIL* RM18.................8 D4
Sermon Dr *SWLY* BR8..............30 A4
Seven Acres *SWLY* BR8............40 B2
Sexton Rd *TIL* RM18...................8 D3
Seymour Rd *GVW* DA11...........17 H5
*DA11...8 D3
Seymour Wk *SWCM* DA10 ....16 A4
Shaftesbury La *DART* DA1........13 H1
Shakespeare Av *TIL* RM18..........9 F4
Shakespeare Rd *DART* DA1.......13 G1
Shamrock Rd *GVE* DA12...........19 E4
Sharland Rd *GVE* DA12.............27 G1
Sharp Wy *DART* DA1...................4 B5
Shaw Crs *TIL* RM18....................9 F3
Shearwater *HART* DA3..............35 H4
Shearwood Crs *DART* DA1..........2 D5
Shellbank La *RDART* DA2..........24 B4
Shelley Pl *TIL* RM18...................9 F3
Shenley Rd *DART* DA1 ....13 G3
Shepherds La *DART* DA1..........12 A5
Shepherd St *GVW* DA11...........17 F4
Sheppey Cl *ERITH* DA8...............3 F2
Sheppy Pl *GVE* DA12.................18 B4
Sherbourne Cl *BGR/WK* TN15...50 C4
Sherbrooke Cl *BXLYHN* DA7 .....10 C1
Sherfield Rd *GRAYS* RM17..........7 H1
Sheridan Ct *DART* DA1 ....13 G1
Ship La *SWLY* BR8....................31 H2
Shipley Hills Rd *MEO* DA13 .....46 D4
Shirehall Rd *RDART* DA2..........21 H4
Shirley Cl *DART* DA1.................12 C1
DART DA1...28 D1
The Shore *GVW* DA11..............17 E2
Shorne Ifield Rd *GVE* DA12......28 D5
Shrubbery Rd *EYN* DA4............33 F2
GVE DA12...18 B5
Shurlock Av *SWLY* BR8.............30 B3
Shuttlemead *BXLY* DA5............10 B4
Shuttle Rd *DART* DA1.................3 E5
Sibley Cl *BXLYHS* DA6..............10 A2
The Sidings *MEO* * DA13..........47 E1
Silver Birch Cl *RDART* DA2.......20 C3
Silverdale *HART* DA3................35 F5
Silverlocke Rd *GRAYS* RM17......8 B1
Silver Rd *GVE* DA12 ....28 A1
Sinclair Wy *RDART* DA2 ....23 F3
Singlewell Rd *GVW* DA11.........27 F2
Sirdar Strd *GVE* DA12...............28 B4
Skinney La *EYN* DA4.................33 F4
Skippers Cl *GRH* DA9...............15 F2
Slade Gdns *ERITH* DA8...............2 D5
Slade Green Rd *ERITH* DA8........2 D3
Sloane Sq *HART* * DA3..............35 E4
Small Grains *HART* DA3............51 F1
Smarts Rd *GVE* DA12................27 F2
Smuggers Whf *GRH* DA9..........15 F2
Smythe Rd *EYN* DA4.................32 C2
Snelling Av *GVW* DA11.............26 D1
Snipe Cl *ERITH* DA8....................3 F2
Sole St *MEO* DA13....................47 H1
Somerset Rd *DART* DA1 ....12 B3
Somerville Rd *DART* DA1..........13 F3
Sorrell Wy *GVW* DA11..............26 C3
Sounds Ldg *SWLY* BR8.............40 A2
South Ash Rd *BGR/WK* TN15....52 A4
Southern Pl *SWLY* BR8.............30 B5
Southey Wk *TIL* RM18................9 F3
Southfields Rd *BGR/WK* TN15...50 D5
Southfleet Av *HART* DA3...........35 H3
Southfleet Rd *GVW* DA11..........17 H5
RDART DA2.....................................24 C3
SWCM DA10....................................16 C4
South Hall Cl *EYN* DA4.............42 B3
South Hill Rd *GVE* DA12...........18 B5
South Kent Av *GVW* DA11........17 E3
South Rd *ERITH* DA8...................2 C1
South St *GVE* DA12...................18 B4
MEO DA13.......................................53 H2
South Ter *EYN* * DA4................42 B3
South View *TIL* RM18..................9 E3
South View Cl *BXLY* DA5..........10 D3
Southview Cl *SWLY* BR8...........31 E5
South View Hts *WTHK* * RM20 ...6 A1
South View Rd *RDART* DA2.......21 H2
WTHK RM20......................................6 A1
South Wharf Rd *GRAYS* RM17....7 F1
Southwold Rd *BXLY* DA5..........10 D3
Sparepenny La *EYN* DA4...........42 A3
Speedgate Hl *HART* DA3...........44 A5
Spencer St *GVW* DA11.............18 A4
Spencer Wk *TIL* RM18................9 F3
Spielman Rd *DART* DA1............13 F1
Spindles *TIL* RM18......................9 E2
The Spinney *SWLY* BR8............30 C3
Spire Cl *GVE* DA12...................18 B5

The Spires *DART* DA1...............21 H1
Spital St *DART* DA1...................12 D3
Springcroft *HART* DA3..............45 G3
Springfield Av *SWLY* BR8.........30 B3
Spring Cross *HART* DA3............52 B1
Spring Gv *GVE* DA12.................18 B5
Springhead Rd *ERITH* DA8..........2 D1
GVW DA11 ....17 E4
Spring V *BXLYHN* DA7..............10 D1
GRH DA9...15 G3
Spring Vale Cl *SWLY* BR8.........30 D1
Springvale Ct *GVW* * DA11......26 A1
Spring V North *DART* DA1 ....12 D4
Spring V South *DART* * DA1.....12 D4
Sprucedale Cl *SWLY* BR8..........30 C3
Spurrell Av *RDART* DA2............20 B3
The Square *SWLY* * BR8............30 B4
Squires Fld *SWLY* BR8..............31 E2
Squires Wy *RDART* DA2............20 B3
Stacey Cl *GVE* DA12.................28 A4
Stacklands Cl *BGR/WK* TN15....50 C4
Stack La *HART* DA3..................45 F1
Stack Rd *EYN* DA4....................33 F5
Stadium Wy *DART* DA1.............11 H3
Stafford Cl *DART* DA1................4 D3
Stanbrook Rd *DART* DA1..........17 H5
Standard Rd *BXLYHS* DA6 ....10 A1
Stanham Pl *DART* DA1..............12 A1
Stanham Rd *DART* DA1.............12 C2
Stanhope Rd *SWCM* DA10........16 B2
Stanley Cl *GRH* DA9.................14 C2
Stanley Crs *GVE* DA12..............27 H4
Stanley Rd *GRAYS* RM17............7 H1
SWCM DA10....................................16 B3
Stanley Ter *BXLYHS* * DA6........10 C1
Staple Cl *BXLY* DA5..................20 B2
Starboard Av *GRH* DA9............15 G3
Star Hl *DART* DA1.....................11 G2
Starling Cl *HART* DA3...............35 H4
Station Ap *BXLYHN* DA7............2 A4
DART DA1...13 E3
SWLY BR8...30 C5
Station Approach Rd *TIL* RM18...18 A1
Station Rd *DART* DA1................11 H3
EYN DA4...32 D3
EYN DA4...48 D1
GRH DA9...15 E2
GVW DA11 ....16 D3
HART DA3...35 E3
MEO DA13.......................................33 H5
MEO DA13.......................................47 E1
SWLY BR8...30 C5
Stedman Cl *BXLY* DA5 ....15 E2
Steele Av *GRH* DA9..................15 E2
Steele's La *MEO* DA13 ....53 H2
Stelling Rd *ERITH* DA8................2 B2
Stephen Rd *BXLYHN* DA7...........2 A5
Stephenson Av *TIL* RM18...........9 E3
Sterndale Rd *DART* DA1 ....13 F4
Stevens Cl *BXLY* DA5................20 B3
RDART DA2.....................................23 G4
Stevenson Cl *ERITH* DA8............3 F2
Stock La *RDART* DA2................21 C3
Stonebridge Rd *GVW* DA11......16 C2
Stonecroft Rd *ERITH* DA8...........2 A2
Stoneness Rd *WTHK* RM20.........6 B1
Stone Place Rd *GRH* DA9..........14 C2
Stones Cross Rd *SWLY* BR8......40 A1
Stone St *GVE* DA12...................18 B3
Stonewood *RDART* DA2............24 C2
Stony Cnr *HART* DA3................36 C5
Stornaway Strd *GVE* DA12........28 B3
Stour Rd *DART* DA1....................3 E5
Strand Cl *MEO* DA13................47 E3
Strawberry Flds *SWLY* DRO.......30 C3
The Street *BGR/WK* TN15..........52 A4
EYN DA4...32 D5
GVE DA12...29 G4
GVE DA12...38 C5
MEO DA13.......................................47 G4
Strickland Av *DART* DA1 ....4 D1
Struttons Av *GVW* DA11...........26 D1
Stuart Cl *SWLY* BR8..................30 D4
Stuart Mantle Wy *ERITH* DA8.....2 B2
Stuart Rd *GVW* DA11................18 A3
Studley Crs *HART* DA3.............36 A3
Suffolk Rd *DART* DA1...............13 E3
GVE DA12...18 D3
Sullivan Cl *DART* DA1...............12 B3
Sullivan Rd *TIL* RM18..................9 E3
Summerhill Rd *DART* DA1.........12 D4
Summerhouse Dr *RDART* DA2...20 B1
Sun Ct *ERITH* DA8......................2 D1
Sundridge Cl *DART* DA1 ....13 G3
Sun Hl *HART* DA3.....................45 A5
Sunland Av *BXLYHS* DA6..........10 A1
Sun La *GVE* DA12......................27 G1
Sunninghill *GVW* DA11.............26 C1

Sun Rd SWCM DA10......16 B3
Sunset CI ERITH DA8......3 F2
Surrey CI BGR/WK * TN15......50 C5
Sussex CI BGR/WK * TN15......50 C5
Sussex Rd DART DA1......13 G4
Sutherland CI GVE DA12......28 D1
Swaisland Rd DART DA1......12 B2
Swaislands Dr DART DA1......11 H2
Swaledale Rd RDART DA2......14 A5
Swale Rd DART DA1......3 E5
Swallow CI BXLYHN DA7......2 C3
  GRH DA9......14 D2
Swan La DART DA1......11 H4
Swanley La SWLY BR8......30 D4
Swanley Village Rd SWLY BR8......31 F2
Swanscombe St SWCM DA10......16 B3
Sweyne Rd SWCM DA10......16 A3
Swiller's La GVE DA12......29 G4
Swinburne Gdns TIL RM18......9 F4
Sycamore CI GVE DA12......18 D4
  TIL RM18......8 D3
Sycamore Dr SWLY BR8......30 C4
Sycamore Rd DART DA1......12 C4
Sydney Rd TIL RM18......9 E4
Symonds CI BGR/WK TN15......50 C3

T

Tallents CI EYN DA4......32 D1
Tamesis Strd GVE DA12......28 A4
Tanyard HI GVE DA12......29 C5
Tan Yard La BXLY * DA5......10 C4
Tates Orch HART DA3......45 F2
Taunton CI BXLYHN DA7......2 B3
Taunton Rd GVW DA11......16 C2
Taunton V GVE DA12......27 H2
Taylor Rw RDART DA2......21 G2
Teesdale Rd RDART DA2......14 A5
Templar Dr GVW DA11......27 E4
Templars Ct DART * DA1......13 G2
Temple HI DART DA1......13 F2
Temple Hill Sq DART DA1......13 F2
Tennants Rw TIL * RM18......8 C4
Tennyson Rd DART DA1......13 G2
Tennyson Wk GVW DA11......26 B2
  TIL RM18......9 F4
Tensing Av GVW * DA11......26 C2
Terence CI GVE DA12......28 B1
The Terraces RDART DA2......14 A4
Terrace St GVE DA12......18 B3
The Terrace GVE DA12......18 B3
  GVE * DA12......38 B4
Thackeray Av TIL RM18......9 G3
Thames Ga DART DA1......13 G2
Thames Rd DART DA1......3 E5
  GRAYS RM17......7 H2
Thames Wy GVW DA11......17 F5
Thanet Rd BXLY DA5......10 C4
  ERITH DA8......2 C2
Thelma CI GVE DA12......28 B4
Third Av GVW * DA11......17 H5
  WTHK RM20......6 A1
Thirlmere Rd BXLYHN DA7......2 A4
Thirza Rd DART DA1......13 F3
Thistle Rd GVE DA12......19 E4
Thomas Dr GVE DA12......27 H1
Thong La GVE DA12......28 C5
  GVE DA12......28 B2
Three Gates Rd HART DA3......44 A3
The Thrift RDART DA2......24 C2
Thurrock Park Wy GRAYS RM17 ......8 B2
Thwaite CI RDART DA2......2 A1
Tilbury Gdns TIL RM18......18 A1
Tile Kiln La BXLY DA5......20 B1
Till Av EYN DA4......42 B3
Tilmans Md EYN DA4......42 B3
Timothy CI BXLYHS DA6......10 A2
Tollgate Rd RDART DA2......14 B4
Tooley St GVW DA11......17 F4
Top Dartford Rd SWLY BR8......21 E5
Toronto Rd TIL RM18......9 E4
Torrens Wk GVE DA12......28 A4
Tower CI GVE DA12......28 A4
Tower Cft EYN DA4......42 A5
Tower Park Rd DART DA1......11 H2
Tower Rd BXLYHN DA7......10 D1
  DART DA1......12 C4
Towers Wd EYN DA4......33 F2
Tower Whf GVW * DA11......16 D1
Townfield Cnr GVE DA12......18 C5
Townley Rd BXLYHS DA6......10 B4
Town Square Crs GRH DA9......14 D4
Tradescant Dr MEO DA13......47 F2
Trafalgar Rd DART DA1......22 A1
  GVW DA11......18 A4
Trebble Rd SWCM DA10......16 A3
Tredegar Rd RDART DA2......21 E2
Treetops GVE DA12......27 F4

Trevelyan CI DART DA1......13 F1
Trevithick Dr DART DA1......13 F1
Trinity Gdns DART DA1......12 D3
Trinity PI BXLYHS DA6......10 B1
Trinity Rd GVE DA12......18 C4
Trivett CI GRH DA9......15 E2
Trolling Down HI RDART DA2......22 D1
Trosley Av GVW DA11......27 F1
Truro Rd GVE DA12......27 H2
Tudor CI DART DA1......12 B3
  GVW DA11......17 G5
Tudor Ct SWLY BR8......40 A3
Tufnail Rd DART DA1......13 F3
Turnbull CI RDART DA2......14 C4
Turner Ct DART DA1......12 C2
Turner Rd RDART DA2......24 B2
Turner's Oak Shaw HART DA3......45 E5
Turners PI EYN * DA4......33 E2
Turnstone HART DA3......35 G4
The Turnstones GVE DA12......27 H1
Turpin La ERITH DA8......3 E1
Twigg CI DART DA1......2 C2
Twisleton Ct DART DA1......12 D3
Tylers Green Rd SWLY BR8......40 A2
Tynedale CI RDART DA2......14 B5
Tyrrells Hall CI GRAYS RM17......8 B1

U

Unicorn Wk GRH DA9......14 D2
University Gdns BXLY DA5......10 B4
University Wy DART DA1......3 H5
Upper Austin Lodge Rd
  EYN DA4......48 D3
Upper Av MEO DA13......36 C2
Upton CI BXLY DA5......10 B3
Upton Rd BXLYHS DA6......10 A1
Upton Rd South BXLY DA5......10 B3

V

Valence Rd ERITH DA8......2 B2
Vale Rd DART DA1......12 B5
  GVW DA11......17 F4
Valley CI DART DA1......11 H3
Valley Dr GVE DA12......27 H2
Valley Gdns GRH DA9......15 F3
Valley Rd DART DA1......11 H3
  HART DA3......44 B4
Valley Vw GRH DA9......15 F3
Valley View Ter EYN * DA4......42 B4
Vanessa Wk GVE DA12......28 B4
Vanessa Wy BXLY DA5......20 B2
Vanquisher Wk GVE DA12......28 B2
Vauxhall CI GVW DA11......17 H4
Vauxhall PI DART DA1......13 E4
Venners CI BXLYHN DA7......2 C4
Venture CI BXLY DA5......10 A4
Vernon Rd SWCM DA10......16 B3
Verona Gdns GVE DA12......28 A3
Viaduct Ter EYN * DA4......33 E3
Via Romana GVE DA12......19 H5
Vicarage CI ERITH DA8......2 A1
Vicarage Dr GVW DA11......17 E3
Vicarage La GVE DA12......28 C1
Vicarage Rd BXLY DA5......10 D5
Vicarage Sq GRAYS RM17......7 G1
Victoria Dr EYN DA4......33 F3
Victoria Hill Rd SWLY BR8......30 D2
Victoria Rd BXLYHS DA6......10 C2
  DART DA1......12 D2
  ERITH DA8......2 C1
  GVW DA11......17 H5
Victory Wy GRH DA9......14 A1
  RDART * DA2......14 A4
Vigilant Wy GVE DA12......28 B4
Viking Rd GVW DA11......26 A2
Viking Wy BGR/WK TN15......50 C3
Villa CI GVE DA12......28 D1
Village Green Rd DART DA1......12 A1
Volante Wy GVE DA12......28 A3

W

Wadard Ter SWLY * BR8......41 G1
Waid CI DART DA1......13 F3
Wakefield Rd GRH DA9......15 G2
Waldeck Rd DART DA1......13 F4
Walker CI DART DA1......2 D5
Walkley Rd DART DA1......12 B2
Wallace Gdns SWCM DA10......16 A3
Wallhouse Rd ERITH DA8......3 G2
Wallis CI RDART DA2......21 E1
Walnut Hill Rd MEO DA13......36 C4

Walnut Tree Av DART DA1......22 A1
Walnut Tree Wy MEO DA13......47 E2
Walnut Wy SWLY BR8......30 B3
Waltham Rd DART DA1......12 A3
Wansbury Wy SWLY BR8......41 E1
Wansunt Rd BXLY DA5......11 E5
Ward CI ERITH DA8......2 B1
Warren CI BXLYHS DA6......10 C2
Warren Rd BXLYHS DA6......10 C2
  DART DA1......22 A2
  MEO DA13......25 H4
The Warrens HART DA3......45 F2
The Warren GVE DA12......27 H3
Warren Vw GVE DA12......29 C4
Warrior Av GVE DA12......27 G3
Warwick CI BXLY DA5......10 B4
Warwick Gdns MEO DA13......47 E5
Warwick PI GVW DA11......16 D2
Waterdales GVW DA11......17 F5
Waterhead CI ERITH DA8......2 C2
Waterloo St GVE DA12......18 C4
Watermeadow CI ERITH DA8......3 F2
Water Mill Wy EYN DA4......32 D3
Waterside DART DA1......11 G2
Waterton Av GVE DA12......19 E4
Watling St BXLYHS DA6......10 D1
  DART DA1......13 H4
  GVE DA12......38 C2
  GVW DA11......27 F4
  MEO DA13......25 H2
Watson CI WTHK RM20......6 A3
Waylands SWLY BR8......30 D5
Wayville Rd DART DA1......13 H4
Weald CI MEO DA13......36 C1
Wealdway MEO DA13......27 F5
Weardale Av RDART DA2......23 E1
Weavers CI GVW DA11......18 A5
Webber CI ERITH DA8......3 F2
Weird Wd HART DA3......36 A4
Weir Rd BXLY DA5......10 D4
Wellcome Av DART DA1......13 E1
Well Fld HART DA3......35 F5
Wellington Rd DART DA1......12 C3
  TIL RM18......9 E4
Wellington St GVE DA12......18 C4
Wentworth CI GVW DA11......27 E4
Wentworth Dr DART DA1......12 A4
Wessex Dr ERITH DA8......2 C4
Westcott Av GVW DA11......27 E2
Westcourt Pde GVE * DA12......28 B2
West Crescent Rd GVE DA12......18 B3
Wested La SWLY BR8......41 E3
Western Cross CI GRH DA9......15 C3
Westfield CI GVE DA12......27 G5
Westfield Rd BXLYHN DA7......2 A5
Westgate Rd DART DA1......12 D3
Westharold SWLY BR8......30 B4
West Heath CI DART * DA1......11 H3
West Heath Rd DART DA1......11 H3
West HI DART DA1......12 D3
Westhill CI GVE DA12......18 B5
West Hill Dr DART DA1......12 D3
West Hill Ri DART DA1......12 D3
West Holme ERITH DA8......2 A3
West Kent Av GVW DA11......17 E3
West MI GVW DA11......17 H5
West Shaw HART DA3......34 D3
West St BXLYHN DA7......10 B1
  GRAYS RM17......7 G1
  GVW DA11......17 G1
West View Rd DART DA1......13 F3
  SWLY BR8......31 E5
  SWLY BR8......40 B2
Westwood Rd MEO DA13......25 H4
West Woodside BXLY DA5......10 A5
Wharfedale Rd RDART DA2......14 A5
Wharf Rd GRAYS RM17......7 F1
  GVE DA12......19 E3
The Wharf GRH * DA9......15 F1
Wheatley CI GVE DA12......15 E2
Wheatley Terrace Rd ERITH DA8......2 D1
Whenman Av BXLY DA5......20 A1
Whinfell Wy GVE DA12......28 B3
Whitby CI DART DA1......12 B2
White Av GVW DA11......26 C2
Whitecroft SWLY BR8......30 C3
Whitegates Av BGR/WK TN15......50 C4
Whitehall La ERITH DA8......2 D4
  GRAYS RM17......8 A1
White Hart Yd GVE * DA12......18 C3
Whitehead CI RDART DA2......21 G2
Whitehill La GVE DA12......27 H2
Whitehill Pde GVE DA12......27 G2
Whitehill Rd DART DA1......12 A2
  GVE DA12......27 G1
  MEO DA13......36 D1
White Oak Sq SWLY * BR8......30 C4
White Post HI EYN DA4......42 D3
White Post La MEO DA13......37 F5
Whites CI GRH DA9......15 G3
Wickhams Wy HART DA3......45 F1

Wicksteed CI BXLY DA5
Widgeon Rd ERITH DA8
Wilberforce Wy GVE DA12
Wilde CI TIL RM18
Wilfred St GVE DA12
Wilks Av DART DA1
William St GRAYS RM17
  GVE DA12
Willow Av SWLY BR8
Willow CI BXLY DA5
Willow Rd DART DA1
  ERITH DA8
The Willows GRAYS RM17
Willow Ter EYN * DA4
Willow Wk DART * DA1
  MEO DA13
Wilmington Court Rd
  RDART DA2
Wilmot Rd DART DA1
Wilson La EYN DA4
Wilsons Wy MEO DA13
Wiltshire CI DART DA1
Winchester Crs GVE DA12
Windermere CI DART DA1
Windermere Rd BXLYHN DA7
Windhover Wy GVE DA12
Windmill St GVE DA12
Windsor Dr DART DA1
Windsor Rd BXLYHS DA6
  GVE DA12
Wingfield Rd GVW DA11
Winifred Rd DART DA1
Winston CI GRH DA9
Wise's La BGR/WK TN15
Wisteria Gdns SWLY BR8
Wodehouse Rd DART DA1
Wolsley CI DART DA1
Wombwell Gdns GVW DA11
Woodberry Gv BXLY DA5
Wood CI BXLY DA5
Wood End SWLY BR8
Woodfall Dr DART DA1
Woodfield Av GVW DA11
Woodgers Gv SWLY BR8
Woodland Av HART DA3
Woodland CI HART DA3
Woodland CI SWLY BR8
Woodlands La GVE DA12
Woodlands Pk BXLY DA5
Woodlands Ri SWLY BR8
Woodlands Ter SWLY * BR8
Woodland Wy GRH DA9
Wood La RDART DA2
Woodlea HART DA3
Woodmount SWLY BR8
Woodside CI BXLYHN DA7
Woodside Dr RDART DA2
Woodside Rd BXLYHN DA7
Woodstock CI BXLY DA5
Wood St GRAYS RM17
  SWLY BR8
Woodview RDART * DA2
Wood View CI BGR/WK TN15
Woodview Rd SWLY BR8
Woodville Cottages GVE * DA12
Woodville PI GVE DA12
Woodward Ter GRH DA9
Woollett CI DART DA1
Worcester CI GRH DA9
  MEO DA13
Wordsworth CI TIL RM18
Wordsworth Wy DART DA1
Wouldham Rd WTHK RM20
Wrens Cft GVW DA11
Wren Wk TIL RM18
Wrotham Rd GVW DA11
  MEO DA13
Wyatt Rd DART DA1
Wycliffe Rw GVW DA11
Wye Rd GVE DA12
Wykeham CI GVE DA12
Wyvern CI DART DA1

Y

The Yews GVE DA12
Yew Tree CI HART DA3
York PI GRAYS RM17
York Rd DART DA1
  GVE DA12
  GVW DA11
York Ter ERITH DA8

Z

Zion PI GVW DA11

RT DA1 .... 13 E4
nema
E DA12 .... 18 B3
Industrial Park
RT DA1 .... 11 H3
Trading Centre
HK RM20 .... 6 D1
Education Centre
RT DA1 .... 13 F4
r Bay Industrial Estate
TH DA8 .... 2 D2
Centre
RT DA1 .... 13 E3
ea Centre
RT DA1 .... 18 B3
ny Roper Primary School
N DA4 .... 42 A5
entre
E DA12 .... 18 B3
Chase School
RT DA3 .... 35 F4
urst Primary School
YHN DA7 .... 2 A3
urst Public Pay & Play
Club
YHN DA7 .... 2 B5
Cray Primary School
T DA1 .... 12 A1
rimary School
RT DA2 .... 24 C2
Sports Centre
E DA12 .... 12 C3
roft Farm
ustrial Estate
/WK TN15 .... 51 H1
y Street
ustrial Estate
E DA12 .... 18 C3
Cricket Club
Y DA5 .... 10 C5
Erith Technical
School
Y DA5 .... 10 C3
heath Centre
HS DA6 .... 10 A1
heath Golf Club
HS DA6 .... 10 A2
Hospital
DA5 .... 20 C1
RFC
DA5 .... 10 C4
ood County
ary School
Y BR8 .... 30 B2
ood Park Golf Club
RT DA2 .... 30 A1
alet Industrial Park
/WK TN15 .... 50 B4
er Park
DA9 .... 14 D4
Road Industrial Park
T DA1 .... 11 F2
Industrial Centre
DA13 .... 53 H2
Hatch
r Racing Circuit
DA3 .... 50 D2
nt Primary School
T DA2 .... 14 A4
view Industrial Estate
K RM20 .... 6 A1
y Shopping Centre
HS DA6 .... 10 C1
ay Square
ping Centre
HN DA7 .... 10 C1
chool
DA11 .... 18 A4
n Trading Estate
DA1 .... 12 D1
ark Country Park
DA13 .... 47 G3
dustrial Park
A12 .... 18 D3
s Leisure Centre
A12 .... 28 C3
d Primary School
A11 .... 17 H5
Park Arena
DA1 .... 13 E5
Primary School
A12 .... 18 C4
rading Estate
A8 .... 3 E2
d Cinema
S DA6 .... 10 D1

Civic Centre & Woodville Halls
GVW DA11 .... 18 B4
Clearways Industrial Estate
BGR/WK TN15 .... 50 C5
Cobham Primary School
GVE DA12 .... 38 C4
Colyers Lane Medical Centre
BXLYHN DA7 .... 2 B3
Colyers Primary School
BXLYHN DA7 .... 2 B3
Convent Preparatory School
GVE DA12 .... 27 C1
Corinthian Sports Club
HART DA3 .... 44 D2
Crayford Commercial Centre
DART DA1 .... 11 C2
Crayford Industrial Estate
DART DA1 .... 11 H2
Crayford Leisure Centre &
Greyhound Stadium
DART DA1 .... 11 C3
Crayford Medical Centre
DART DA1 .... 11 H2
Crayside Industrial Estate
DART DA1 .... 3 E5
Crockenhill Primary School
SWLY BR8 .... 40 A2
Culverstone Green
Primary School
MEO DA13 .... 53 G5
Cygnet Leisure Centre
GVW DA11 .... 26 C1
Darenth Primary School
RDART DA2 .... 23 H5
Darent Valley Hospital
RDART DA2 .... 14 B5
Dartford County Court
DART DA1 .... 13 E3
Dartford FC
EYN DA4 .... 32 C2
RDART DA2 .... 13 H5
Dartford Golf Club
DART DA1 .... 21 F1
Dartford Grammar
School for Boys
DART DA1 .... 12 C4
Dartford Grammar
School for Girls
DART DA1 .... 12 C4
Dartford Hospital School
HART DA3 .... 35 G4
Dartford Magistrates Court
DART DA1 .... 12 D3
Dartford Museum & Library
DART DA1 .... 13 E4
Dartford Natural Health Centre
DART DA1 .... 13 E4
Dartford Tunnel
DART DA1 .... 5 F3
Dartford West Health Centre
DART DA1 .... 12 C3
Dartford West
Technology College
DART DA1 .... 12 C4
Dominoes Health Centre
GRAYS RM17 .... 7 G1
Dover Road Primary School
GVW DA11 .... 17 G5
Downsview Infant School
SWLY BR8 .... 31 E4
Ebbsfleet Industrial Estate
GVW DA11 .... 16 C2
Erith & District Hospital
ERITH DA8 .... 2 B1
Erith Health Centre
ERITH DA8 .... 2 C1
Erith School
ERITH DA8 .... 2 A2
Erith Small Business Centre
ERITH DA8 .... 2 D1
Erith Sports Centre
ERITH DA8 .... 2 C1
Erith Stadium
ERITH DA8 .... 2 C1
Eynsford Castle
EYN DA4 .... 42 A5
Eynsford Cricket Club
EYN DA4 .... 42 A5
Fairfield Pool & Leisure Centre
DART DA1 .... 13 E4
Farningham Woods
(Nature Reserve)
SWLY BR8 .... 31 H5
Fawkham CE Primary School
HART DA3 .... 44 A4
Fawkham Manor Hospital
HART DA3 .... 44 C4

Fleetdown Primary School
RDART DA2 .... 23 E1
Fleetway Sports Club
GVE DA12 .... 18 C5
Furness School
SWLY BR8 .... 20 D5
Furness Swanley FC
SWLY BR8 .... 40 B1
Galley Hill Industrial Estate
SWCM DA10 .... 16 A2
Geoffrey Whitworth Theatre
DART DA1 .... 12 A1
Globe Industrial Estate
GRAYS RM17 .... 8 A1
Gravel Hill Primary School
BXLYHS DA6 .... 10 D2
Gravesend County Court
GVE DA12 .... 18 B3
Gravesend Cricket Club
GVW DA11 .... 18 A4
Gravesend Grammar School
GVE DA12 .... 18 D4
Gravesend Grammar
School for Girls
GVW DA11 .... 18 A5
Gravesend Museum
GVW DA11 .... 18 B3
Gravesend & Northfleet FC
GVW DA11 .... 17 E3
Gravesend & North Kent Hospital
GVW DA11 .... 18 A3
Gravesend Rowing Club
GVE DA12 .... 18 C3
Gravesend Yacht Club
GVE DA12 .... 18 D3
Grays Athletic FC
GRAYS RM17 .... 7 H1
Grays County Court
GRAYS RM17 .... 7 G1
Greenhithe Health Clinic
GRH DA9 .... 15 F2
Guru Nanak Sports Club
GVE DA12 .... 18 C4
Hall Place
BXLY DA5 .... 11 E3
Hartley Primary School
HART DA3 .... 45 E1
Helen Alison School
MEO DA13 .... 47 E3
Hextable Comprehensive School
SWLY BR8 .... 30 D2
Hextable Primary School
SWLY BR8 .... 20 D5
High Firs Primary School
SWLY BR8 .... 30 D5
Holy Trinity CE Primary School
DART DA1 .... 12 C2
GVE DA12 .... 18 C4
Horns Cross
GRH DA9 .... 14 D3
Horton Kirby CE
Primary School
EYN DA4 .... 33 E4
Horton Kirby Trading Estate
EYN DA4 .... 33 E5
Ifield School
GVE DA12 .... 27 G4
Imperial Business Estate
GVW DA11 .... 17 H3
Imperial Retail Park
GVW DA11 .... 18 A3
Industrial Estate
DART DA1 .... 13 F2
Invicta Sports Club
DART DA1 .... 12 D2
Istead Rise Primary School
MEO DA13 .... 36 C2
Jack Lobley Primary School
TIL RM18 .... 8 D3
Joydens Wood Infant School
RDART DA2 .... 20 C3
Joydens Wood Junior School
BXLY DA5 .... 20 C3
Kent Kraft Industrial Estate
GVW DA11 .... 16 B1
Kestner Industrial Estate
GRH DA9 .... 15 E2
Kings Farm Infant School
GVE DA12 .... 27 G4
Kings Farm Junior School
GVE DA12 .... 27 G3
Langafel CE Primary School
HART DA3 .... 35 G4
Lansdowne Primary School
TIL RM18 .... 8 D2
Lawn Primary School
GVW DA11 .... 17 E3

The Leigh City
Technology College
DART DA1 .... 13 G5
Lesney Park Primary School
ERITH DA8 .... 2 B1
Leyton Cross
DART DA1 .... 21 E1
Littlebrook Business Centre
DART DA1 .... 5 E5
Livingstone Hospital
DART DA1 .... 13 F4
The London Golf Club
BGR/WK TN15 .... 51 G5
London International
Cruise Terminal
TIL RM18 .... 18 A1
Lowfield Medical Centre
DART DA1 .... 13 E4
Lullingstone Castle
EYN DA4 .... 48 C3
Lullingstone Roman Villa
EYN DA4 .... 48 B3
Manford Industrial Estate
ERITH DA8 .... 3 F1
Manor Way Industrial Estate
GRAYS RM17 .... 8 A2
Manzoori Clinic
SWLY BR8 .... 30 D1
Matrix Business Centre
DART DA1 .... 13 E2
May Avenue Industrial Estate
GVW DA11 .... 17 H5
Mayplace Primary School
BXLYHN DA7 .... 11 F1
Maypole Primary School
BXLY DA5 .... 20 C1
Meopham CP School
MEO DA13 .... 47 E3
Meopham Medical Centre
MEO DA13 .... 47 E5
Meopham School
MEO DA13 .... 47 E5
Mid Kent Golf Club
GVW DA11 .... 27 F2
Milestone School
HART DA3 .... 45 F4
Millside Industrial Estate
DART DA1 .... 12 D1
Milton Road Business Park
GVE DA12 .... 18 C4
Moreton Industrial Estate
SWLY BR8 .... 31 F5
New Ash Green
Primary School
HART DA3 .... 45 E4
Normandy Primary School
BXLYHN DA7 .... 2 B3
Northcourt Primary School
GVE DA12 .... 19 E5
Northend Primary School
ERITH DA8 .... 2 D3
North End Trading Estate
ERITH DA8 .... 2 C2
Northfleet Cemetery
GVW DA11 .... 17 E5
Northfleet Industrial Estate
GVW DA11 .... 16 B1
Northfleet School for Boys
GVW DA11 .... 17 F5
Northfleet School for Girls
GVW DA11 .... 26 B1
Northumberland Heath
Medical Centre
ERITH DA8 .... 2 B2
North West Kent College of
Technology
DART DA1 .... 12 C4
GVE DA12 .... 19 F5
Oakfield Primary School
DART DA1 .... 21 H1
Old Bexley Business Park
BXLY DA5 .... 10 C4
Old Bexley CE Primary School
BXLY DA5 .... 10 B5
The Old Guild Theatre
GVW DA11 .... 17 F5
Orchard Shopping Centre
DART DA1 .... 13 E3
The Orchard Theatre
DART DA1 .... 13 E3
Our Lady of Hartley RC
Primary School
HART DA3 .... 45 F1
Our Ladys Catholic
Primary School
DART DA1 .... 12 C3
Painters Ash Primary School
GVW DA11 .... 26 B2

Parker Industrial Centre
RDART DA2 .... **14** A4
Park Road Industrial Estate
SWLY BR8 .... **30** D4
Parkwood Hall School
SWLY BR8 .... **31** F4
Pedham Place Industrial Estate
SWLY BR8 .... **41** E1
Power Industrial Estate
ERITH DA8 .... **2** D3
Priory Shopping Centre
DART DA1 .... **12** D3
Raynehurst Junior School
GVE DA12 .... **28** B2
Regional Sports Centre
TIL RM18 .... **9** F4
Riverside Industrial Estate
DART DA1 .... **13** E2
Riverview Clinic
GVE DA12 .... **28** B4
Riverview Primary School
GVE DA12 .... **28** A3
Rochester & Cobham Park
Golf Club
GVE DA12 .... **39** F4
Rosherville CE Primary School
GVW DA11 .... **17** G3
Rowhill School
RDART DA2 .... **21** G3
Royal Terrace Pier
GVE DA12 .... **18** C2
St Albans Road Infant School
DART DA1 .... **13** F3
St Anselms RC Primary School
DART DA1 .... **13** G2
St Bartholomews Hospital
SWLY BR8 .... **30** D4
St Bartholomews RC
Primary School
SWLY BR8 .... **30** C4
St Botolphs CE Primary School
GVW DA11 .... **17** F4
St Catherines RC Girls School
BXLYHS DA6 .... **10** D2
St Chads School
TIL RM18 .... **9** E3
St Columbas RC Boys School
BXLYHS DA6 .... **10** D2

St Fidelis Catholic
Primary School
ERITH DA8 .... **2** A1
St Georges Centre
GVW DA11 .... **18** B3
St Georges CE School
GVW DA11 .... **27** E1
St Johns RC
Comprehensive School
GVE DA12 .... **18** D5
St Johns RC Primary School
GVE DA12 .... **18** D5
St Josephs RC Primary School
DART DA1 .... **11** F1
St Josephs RC School
DART DA1 .... **17** F4
St Marys CE Primary School
SWLY BR8 .... **30** C5
St Marys RC Primary School
TIL RM18 .... **8** D4
St Paulinus CE Primary School
DART DA1 .... **11** G1
St Pauls CE Primary School
SWLY BR8 .... **31** F2
School of Health
RDART DA2 .... **13** H3
Sedleys CE Primary School
MEO DA13 .... **25** G4
Shears Green Primary School
GVW DA11 .... **26** D2
Shenstone School
DART DA1 .... **11** F2
Shorne CE Primary School
GVE DA12 .... **29** G4
Shorne Wood Country Park
GVE DA12 .... **39** E2
Showcase Bluewater Cinema
GRH DA9 .... **14** D5
Singlewell Primary School
GVE DA12 .... **27** H5
Slade Green FC
ERITH DA8 .... **3** F3
Slade Green Primary School
ERITH DA8 .... **3** E2
Southern Valley Golf Club
GVE DA12 .... **28** C3
Southfields School
GVE DA12 .... **27** G4

Stone House Hospital
RDART DA2 .... **14** A3
Super Bowl
BXLYHS DA6 .... **10** B1
Sutton at Hone CE
Primary School
EYN DA4 .... **32** C1
Swan Business Park
DART DA1 .... **12** D1
Swanley School
SWLY BR8 .... **30** B4
Swanscombe Business Centre
SWCM DA10 .... **16** A2
Swan Valley Community School
SWCM DA10 .... **16** B4
The Sweyne Junior School
SWCM DA10 .... **16** B4
TCA Leisure Centre
TIL RM18 .... **9** E4
Teardrop Industrial Park
SWLY BR8 .... **41** G1
Temple Hill Primary School
DART DA1 .... **13** G2
Thameside Primary School
GRAYS RM17 .... **8** A1
Thamesview School
GVE DA12 .... **28** B2
Thurrock Business Centre
WTHK RM20 .... **5** H1
Tilbury Fort
TIL RM18 .... **18** C1
Tilbury/Gravesend
Passenger Ferry
TIL RM18 .... **18** B1
Tilbury Manorjunior School
TIL RM18 .... **9** F2
Tower Retail Park
DART DA1 .... **11** H2
Townley Grammar
School for Girls
RXLYHS DA6 .... **10** B3
Tunnel Industrial Estate
WTHK RM20 .... **5** H1
University of Greenwich
DART DA1 .... **21** G1
DART DA1 .... **22** B1
Upton Day Hospital
BXLYHS DA6 .... **10** A1

Upton Primary School
BXLY DA5 ....
Upton Road School
BXLYHS DA6 ....
Victoria Industrial Park
DART DA1 ....
Wentworth Primary School
DART DA1 ....
Westcourt Primary School
GVE DA12 ....
Westgate Primary School
DART DA1 ....
West Hill Primary School
DART DA1 ....
West Thurrock Primary School
WTHK RM20 ....
Whitehill Junior School
DART DA1 ....
White Oak Primary School
SWLY BR8 ....
Wilmington Boys
Grammar School
RDART DA2 ....
Wilmington Grammar
School for Girls
RDART DA2 ....
Wilmington Hall School
RDART DA2 ....
Wilmington Primary School
RDART DA2 ....
Windmill Business Centre
MEO DA13 ....
World End
TIL RM18 ....
Wrotham Road Health Clinic
GVW DA11 ....
Wrotham Road
Primary School
GVW DA11 ....
York Road Junior School
DART DA1 ....

Notes

QUESTIONNAIRE

Dear Atlas User
Your comments, opinions and recommendations are very important to us.
So please help us to improve our street atlases by taking a few minutes
to complete this simple questionnaire.

You do NOT need a stamp (unless posted outside the UK). If you do not want to remove this page from your street atlas, then photocopy it or write your answers on a plain sheet of paper.

Send to: The Editor, AA Street by Street, FREEPOST SCE 4598,
Basingstoke RG21 4GY

ABOUT THE ATLAS...

Which city/town/county did you buy?

Are there any features of the atlas or mapping that you find particularly useful?

Is there anything we could have done better?

Why did you choose an AA Street by Street atlas?

Did it meet your expectations?

Exceeded ☐   **Met all** ☐   **Met most** ☐   **Fell below** ☐

Please give your reasons

Where did you buy it?

For what purpose? (please tick all applicable)

To use in your own local area ☐   To use on business or at work ☐

Visiting a strange place ☐   In the car ☐   On foot ☐

Other (please state)

LOCAL KNOWLEDGE...

Local knowledge is invaluable. Whilst every attempt has been made to make the information contained in this atlas as accurate as possible, should you notice any inaccuracies, please detail them below (if necessary, use a blank piece of paper) or e-mail us at *streetbystreet@theAA.com*

ABOUT YOU...

Name (Mr/Mrs/Ms)
Address
                                                        Postcode
Daytime tel no
E-mail address

Which age group are you in?

Under 25 ☐   25-34 ☐   35-44 ☐   45-54 ☐   55-64 ☐   65+ ☐

Are you an AA member?   YES ☐   NO ☐

Do you have Internet access?   YES ☐   NO ☐

Thank you for taking the time to complete this questionnaire. Please send it to us as soon as possible, and remember, you do not need a stamp (unless posted outside the UK).

ML